☑ MAN ENOUGH?

Which one of these actors was *not* a member of the ultra-badass, Nazi-stomping assault team The Dirty Dozen?

Ⓐ Strother Martin   Ⓒ Donald Sutherland

Ⓑ Charles Bronson   Ⓓ Telly Savalas

TEST YOUR TESTICULAR
APTITUDE WITH

-HUNDREDS OF- CHALLENGING QUESTIONS

MAN ENOUGH?

THE **FACTS** AND **STATS** EVERY REAL GUY SHOULD KNOW

The first World Series MVP award was handed out in 1955. Who went home with it?

Ⓐ Whitey Ford

Ⓑ Stan Musial

Ⓒ Bob Turley

Ⓓ Johnny Podres

This alcohol is the only liquid the body can consume as food for upwards of thirty days without shutting down.

Ⓐ Vodka

Ⓑ Beer

Ⓒ Wine

Ⓓ Whiskey

MAX BRALLIER AND GEOFF BAKER

Aadamsmedia
Avon, Massachusetts

Published by
Adams Media, a division of F+W Media, Inc.
57 Littlefield Street, Avon, MA 02322. U.S.A.
www.adamsmedia.com

ISBN 10: 1-4405-3338-5
ISBN 13: 978-1-4405-3338-9
eISBN 10: 1-4405-3405-5
eISBN 13: 978-1-4405-3405-8

Printed in the United States of America.

10 9 8 7 6 5 4 3 2 1

Library of Congress Cataloging-in-Publication Data
is available from the publisher.

This publication is designed to provide accurate and authoritative information with regard to the subject matter covered. It is sold with the understanding that the publisher is not engaged in rendering legal, accounting, or other professional advice. If legal advice or other expert assistance is required, the services of a competent professional person should be sought.

—From a *Declaration of Principles* jointly adopted by a Committee of the American Bar Association and a Committee of Publishers and Associations

Many of the designations used by manufacturers and sellers to distinguish their product are claimed as trademarks. Where those designations appear in this book and Adams Media was aware of a trademark claim, the designations have been printed with initial capital letters.

This book is available at quantity discounts for bulk purchases.
For information, please call 1-800-289-0963.

To our dads—a pair of great guys

CONTENTS

INTRODUCTION: THE POINT OF WHOLE THE DAMN THING   9

CHAPTER 1
THE CINEMA: MEN AT THE MOVIES   11

CHAPTER 2
SPORTS: PLAY BALL   41

CHAPTER 3
RATIONS: HOT DOGS, BEER, AND MORE   73

CHAPTER 4
STATS: KNOW YOUR NUMBERS   105

CHAPTER 5
HISTORY: BECAUSE YOU DON'T
WANT TO BE DOOMED TO REPEAT IT   137

CHAPTER 6
TELEVISION: THE BOOB TUBE   169

CHAPTER 7
TRANSPORTATION:
PLANES, TRAINS, AND AUTOMOBILES   199

CHAPTER 8
GENDER RELATIONS: IMPRESSING THE LADIES   229

CHAPTER 9
MISCELLANY:
STUFF YOU SHOULD JUST KNOW, DAMMIT   261

THE FINAL SCORE   293

INDEX   297

THE POINT OF THE WHOLE DAMN THING

What is the point of the book, you ask? The point is to measure your testicular aptitude. What the hell is testicular aptitude? It's sort of an IQ test—for guys. Traditional IQ tests measure a person's abilities in four main categories: memory, language, math, and spatial perception. That's all well and good, and I'm sure your high school math teacher finds it endlessly fascinating, but how often do you, the average (or above-average, if you really want to believe that) Joe need to calculate the area of some crazy triangle? Or need to figure out the square root of 4,922 or know the definition of triptych?

That's why we, your trusted editors, came up with this test of your testicular aptitude. No math, no puzzles, no "spatial perception." We're testing the things that, as a guy, you should just know:

- What type of heat was Clint packing in *Dirty Harry*?
- Bonnie and Clyde were in what kind of car when they were ambushed and shot?
- Which *A-Team* character was played by Mr. T?

In short, are you man enough?

SCORE!

We know you're busy—games to watch, lawns to mow, etc.—so we're making it easy for you. Each chapter has 100 questions. Each question is worth a point. After you've answered all the questions in any particular chapter, flip to the back of the chapter and total up your points. Then, turn to the back of the book to find the final score sheet and tally up your grand total.

Anything 81–100 means you're some sort of godly man super-being. We like the cut of your jib.

61–80 is, as Darth Vader would say, "Impressive."

41–60 means you're an average Joe. Nothing to be ashamed about—but nothing to write home about either.

21–40 is pretty, pretty, *pretty* bad. Hopefully, your other testicle will drop soon.

0–20? Just shameful. Go bury your head in the sand.

Understand the scoring? Good. Now turn the page, start answering some questions, and discover your testicular aptitude!

CHAPTER 1

THE CINEMA: MEN AT THE MOVIES

Before we throw a bunch of questions at you, let's first try to define what a "guy movie" is. There's no one perfect formula, but there are certainly some things that help to make a movie manly and awesome. For starters: gratuitous violence, topless dames, car chases, sniper rifles, explosions, roundhouse kicks, and four-letter words. Also, a little Clint Eastwood or Charles Bronson doesn't hurt. Bottom line: you know a guy movie when you see it. Now let's see if you know your trivia, too.

1. In the 1986 guy movie classic *Top Gun,* what type of fighter jet does Tom Cruise—a.k.a. Maverick—pilot?

   ☐ **a.** F-14 Tomcat
   ☐ **b.** Eagle
   ☐ **c.** F-16 Fighting Falcon
   ☐ **d.** F-18 Hornet

2. Before landing the role of Han Solo in the *Star Wars* movies (the original ones—y'know, the good ones), Harrison Ford busted his butt working as a what?

   ☐ **a.** Carpenter
   ☐ **b.** Car Mechanic
   ☐ **c.** Electrician
   ☐ **d.** Plumber

3. The 1977 sports comedy classic *Slap Shot* featured the three memorable Hanson brothers, played to perfection by the real-life Carlson brothers. But when one brother, Dave Carlson, had to back out due to hockey obligations, this hockey player filled in as the final Hanson brother.

   ☐ **a.** Dave Hanson
   ☐ **b.** John Carlson
   ☐ **c.** Jerry Houser
   ☐ **d.** Andrew Duncan

Top 5 List

Our five favorite sniper scenes:	*Full Metal Jacket* (it was a girl!)
	The Professional (it was fake!)
	Saving Private Ryan (it was amazing!)
	Sniper (it's Berenger!)
	Lethal Weapon (it's Gibson!)

4. Most everyone knows a little something about Tony Montana, the character that Al Pacino brought to vivid, horrifying life in 1980's *Scarface*. Y'know, facts like these: he had piles of blow, loads of money, and firepower aplenty. But do you know what country he hails from?

- ☐ **a.** Italy
- ☐ **b.** Colombia
- ☐ **c.** Panama
- ☐ **d.** Cuba

5. This Hollywood hotshot played the title character in the mob movie *Donnie Brasco*.

- ☐ **a.** Al Pacino
- ☐ **b.** Brad Pitt
- ☐ **c.** Johnny Depp
- ☐ **d.** Robert Downey Jr.

6. Who was the best James Bond? That's easy: Sean Connery. Who was the *worst* James Bond? That's just as easy. Well . . . who was it?

- ☐ **a.** Daniel Craig
- ☐ **b.** Roger Moore
- ☐ **c.** Timothy Dalton
- ☐ **d.** Pierce Brosnan
- ☐ **e.** George Lazenby

7. What gun does Dirty Harry use to clean up the streets and display his general badassness?

- ☐ **a.** Smith and Wesson Model 29 .44 Magnum
- ☐ **b.** Beretta Px4 .45 Caliber
- ☐ **c.** Glock 19 9mm
- ☐ **d.** Smith and Wesson Model 686 .357 Magnum

8. Only once have two actors won an Academy Award for playing the same character. They are both huge stars. Name the character. You better get this one.

☐ **a.** Jack Ryan
☐ **b.** Hannibal Lecter
☐ **c.** Vito Corleone
☐ **d.** The Joker

9. "Yippee-ki-yay Motherfucker" is the tagline of hero John McClane in this classic Bruce Willis movie.

☐ **a.** *The Last Boy Scout*
☐ **b.** *Pulp Fiction*
☐ **c.** *The Fifth Element*
☐ **d.** *Die Hard*

10. This Hollywood legend directed the first two *Terminator* movies.

☐ **a.** Steven Spielberg
☐ **b.** James Cameron
☐ **c.** Michael Bay
☐ **d.** Stanley Kubrick

Classic Quote

"You have to ask yourself one question: Do I feel lucky? Well, do ya, punk?"

—HARRY CALLAHAN, DIRTY HARRY

11. Before *Thunderdome*, there was *The Road Warrior* for this action star.

☐ **a.** Bruce Willis
☐ **b.** Sylvester Stallone
☐ **c.** Mel Gibson
☐ **d.** David Carradine

12. Which one of these actors was *not* a member of the ultra-badass, Nazi-stomping assault team The Dirty Dozen?

- ☐ **a.** Strother Martin
- ☐ **b.** Charles Bronson
- ☐ **c.** Donald Sutherland
- ☐ **d.** Telly Savalas

13. *Matrix* star Keanu Reeves starred alongside Patrick Swayze in this cult action classic.

- ☐ **a.** *Backdraft*
- ☐ **b.** *Surf Ninjas*
- ☐ **c.** *Point Break*
- ☐ **d.** *Johnny Utah and the Great Meatball Sandwich Showdown*

14. What hazardous material does Bill Murray discover at the bottom of the pool in *Caddyshack*?

- ☐ **a.** Dead gopher
- ☐ **b.** Piece of dooky
- ☐ **c.** Cigar
- ☐ **d.** Candy bar

15. Al Pacino and Robert De Niro worked together on *The Godfather Part II*. If you want to see them on opposite sides of the law, check out this 1995 action drama costarring Val Kilmer (before he got all fat and bloated and weird).

- ☐ **a.** *Righteous Kill*
- ☐ **b.** *Miami Takedown*
- ☐ **c.** *Casino*
- ☐ **d.** *Heat*

16. Thanks to *Rocky*, everyone acknowledges "Eye of the Tiger" as the greatest motivational song ever. Hell, pretty much every guy in America has it on his iPod's "gym" playlist. But do you know which band performed it?

☐ **a.** Foreigner
☐ **b.** Journey
☐ **c.** Survivor
☐ **d.** Bad English

17. After proclaiming to his drill sergeant that he was in the Marines "Sir! To kill sir!" what job does Matthew Modine's Joker end up with in *Full Metal Jacket*?

☐ **a.** Sniper
☐ **b.** Infantryman
☐ **c.** Cook
☐ **d.** Reporter

18. One of the best Bond movies of all time (and the first), *Dr. No,* has this actor portraying James Bond.

☐ **a.** Sean Connery
☐ **b.** Roger Moore
☐ **c.** George Lazenby
☐ **d.** Pierce Brosnan

19. Chow Yun-Fat plays a shoot-first, questions-later gunslinger hit man in this signature 1989 John Woo film.

☐ **a.** *Bullet in the Head*
☐ **b.** *The Killer*
☐ **c.** *Hard Target*
☐ **d.** *Broken Arrow*

20. What gritty boxer did Robert De Niro portray in the 1980 classic *Raging Bull*?

☐ **a.** Rocky Marciano
☐ **b.** Jack Johnson
☐ **c.** Jack Dempsey
☐ **d.** Jake LaMotta

True Story
All of the clocks in *Pulp Fiction* are stuck on 4:20.

21. Fact or Fiction: Being the man that he was, Steve McQueen did his own stunt driving for the movie *Bullitt*.

☐ **a.** Fact
☐ **b.** Fiction

22. In the Matrix films, this brilliant character actor, who also appeared in *The Sopranos* as Ralph Cifaretto and *Bad Boys* as Captain Howard, plays Cypher.

☐ **a.** Joe Pantoliano
☐ **b.** Steve Buscemi
☐ **c.** Chris Cooper
☐ **d.** John Turturro

23. Match each Kung Fu legend with the movie he starred in.

☐ **i.** Jackie Chan   **a.** *Enter the Dragon*
☐ **ii.** Bruce Lee   **b.** *Kiss Of the Dragon*
☐ **iii.** Jet Li   **c.** *Ong Bak*
☐ **iv.** Tony Jaa   **d.** *The Legend of the Drunken Master*

24. Which of these mega stars was *not* in Francis Ford Coppola's trippy Vietnam classic *Apocalypse Now*?

☐ **a.** Robert Duvall
☐ **b.** Harrison Ford
☐ **c.** Marlon Brando
☐ **d.** Kirk Douglas

25. This actor played Mr. Pink in *Reservoir Dogs*.

☐ **a.** Michael Madsen
☐ **b.** Tim Roth
☐ **c.** Steve Buscemi
☐ **d.** Harvey Keitel

26. Patrick Swayze and C. Thomas Howell anchored a cast of stars in this 1984 flick with a cold war plot. Fun fact: it was the first film to be rated PG-13.

☐ **a.** *Red Dawn*
☐ **b.** *The Hunt for Red October*
☐ **c.** *Iron Eagle*
☐ **d.** *From Russia with Love*

27. In *Dazed and Confused*, Matthew McConaughey's character spoke this now famous line: "That's what I like about these high school girls. I keep getting older; they stay the same age." His character went by what name?

☐ **a.** Pink
☐ **b.** Wooderson
☐ **c.** Spicoli
☐ **d.** Brigance

28. Fact or Fiction: Several of the cast members from *The Great Escape* were actual POWs in WWII.

☐ **a.** Fact
☐ **b.** Fiction

29. What is the first rule of *Fight Club*?

☐ **a.** No biting, no eye gouging, no fish hooking
☐ **b.** No shirts, no shoes, no punching
☐ **c.** No women in fight club
☐ **d.** You do not talk about fight club

30. This actor played the infamous Keyser Soze in *The Usual Suspects*.

☐ **a.** Benicio Del Toro
☐ **b.** Kevin Pollak
☐ **c.** Kevin Spacey
☐ **d.** Gabriel Byrne

31. At the 1974 world premiere of this film, guests rode into the theater on horseback!

☐ **a.** *The Outlaw Josey Wales*
☐ **b.** *The Longest Yard*
☐ **c.** *Herbie Rides Again*
☐ **d.** *Blazing Saddles*

32. This city provides the setting for the 1941 Humphrey Bogart film noir classic *The Maltese Falcon*.

☐ **a.** New York
☐ **b.** Philadelphia
☐ **c.** Los Angeles
☐ **d.** San Francisco

33. What was the first movie that Clint Eastwood directed but did *not* star in?

☐ **a.** *Play Misty for Me*
☐ **b.** *Breezy*
☐ **c.** *High Plains Drifter*
☐ **d.** *Pale Rider*

34. The 1992 Clint Eastwood/Gene Hackman classic *Unforgiven* was the third Western to do what?

☐ **a.** Run more than two hours
☐ **b.** Break $100 million dollars at the box office
☐ **c.** Win the Oscar for Best Picture
☐ **d.** Feature CGI

35. Which of these actors did *not* appear in the movie *Diner*?

☐ **a.** Paul Reiser
☐ **b.** Robert Downey Jr.
☐ **c.** Kevin Bacon
☐ **d.** Steve Guttenberg

36. In *The Big Lebowski*, The Dude declares a hatred for this band.

☐ **a.** Foreigner
☐ **b.** Wings
☐ **c.** The Beatles
☐ **d.** The Eagles

37. The 1971 blaxploitation classic *Shaft* has one of the most badass theme songs ever. Who wrote and performed it?

☐ **a.** Isaac Hayes
☐ **b.** James Brown
☐ **c.** Al Green
☐ **d.** Barry White

38. Fact or Fiction: *48 Hrs.* was Eddie Murphy's first movie.

☐ **a.** Fact
☐ **b.** Fiction

39. "We've been kicking other people's asses so long, I figure it's about time we got ours kicked" is a great line from which Vietnam flick?

☐ **a.** *Platoon*
☐ **b.** *Apocalypse Now*
☐ **c.** *Born on the Fourth of July*
☐ **d.** *Full Metal Jacket*

40. Which of these is *not* the name of a Bond girl?

☐ **a.** Honey Rider
☐ **b.** Pussy Galore
☐ **c.** Plenty O'Toole
☐ **d.** Chesty Mandolese

41. In *Animal House*, fictional band Otis Day and the Knights (who later toured as a real band!) played which song at the Delta's frat party?

☐ **a.** "I Fought the Law"
☐ **b.** "Shout"
☐ **c.** "I Heard It Through the Grapevine"
☐ **d.** "Hooked on a Feeling"

42. Most guys know Clint Eastwood played "The Good" in *The Good, The Bad, and The Ugly* but who played "The Ugly"?

☐ **a.** Lee Van Cleef
☐ **b.** Eli Wallach
☐ **c.** Gene Hackman
☐ **d.** Rod Steiger

43. Match each actor with the football movie he starred in:

☐ **i.** Burt Reynolds   **a.** *Any Given Sunday*
☐ **ii.** James Caan   **b.** *The Longest Yard*
☐ **iii.** Tom Cruise   **c.** *North Dallas Forty*
☐ **iv.** Denzel Washington   **d.** *Rudy*
☐ **v.** Nick Nolte   **e.** *All the Right Moves*
☐ **vi.** Sean Astin   **f.** *Brian's Song*
☐ **vii.** Jamie Foxx   **g.** *Remember the Titans*

44. In *Stripes*, Bill Murray's career as a cabbie ends pretty quickly. How come?

☐ **a.** He drives *through* Central Park
☐ **b.** He throws a pizza at a passenger
☐ **c.** He abandons his taxi on a bridge
☐ **d.** He drinks while driving

45. Robert De Niro plays a pretty mean Al Capone in *The Untouchables*. But he actually kills only one person during the movie (though it's a doozy!). What was his weapon of choice to take care of business?

☐ **a.** Tommy gun
☐ **b.** Car bomb
☐ **c.** Switchblade
☐ **d.** Baseball bat

46. Which actor played Minnesota Fats opposite Paul Newman in 1961's *The Hustler*?

☐ **a.** Marlon Brando
☐ **b.** Jackie Gleason
☐ **c.** Kirk Douglas
☐ **d.** James Caan

47. What is the name of the detective Gene Hackman plays to perfection in *The French Connection*?

☐ **a.** Popeye Doyle
☐ **b.** George Anderson
☐ **c.** Sam Spade
☐ **d.** Wes Ryan

Did You Know? In *Casablanca* Humphrey Bogart never actually says, "Play it again, Sam."

48. What song do the British POWs famously whistle in *The Bridge on the River Kwai*?

☐ **a.** "The Colonel Bogey March"
☐ **b.** "The Stars and Stripes Forever"
☐ **c.** "The Circus Bee"
☐ **d.** "Old Comrades"

49. In the climax of *Enter the Dragon*, Bruce Lee's kung-fu masterpiece, the villainous Han uses what as a weapon.

☐ **a.** A flaming sword
☐ **b.** Steel claws
☐ **c.** A medieval mace
☐ **d.** Fists dipped in glass

50. "If they move, kill 'em," is a line from this ultra-violent, ultra-awesome Western.

- [ ] **a.** *The Wild Bunch*
- [ ] **b.** *The Good, the Bad, and the Ugly*
- [ ] **c.** *Butch Cassidy and the Sundance Kid*
- [ ] **d.** *The Magnificent Seven*

51. Match the fictional fraternity with the film it appears in

- [ ] **i.** Delta Tau Chi
- [ ] **ii.** Lambda Epsilon Omega
- [ ] **iii.** Lambda Lambda Lambda
- [ ] **iv.** Kappa Lambda
- [ ] **v.** Kappa Omega

a. *Old School*
b. *Dead Man on Campus*
c. *Road Trip*
d. *Animal House*
e. *Revenge of the Nerds*

52. In *Cool Hand Luke*, Paul Newman does the seemingly impossible by eating this many eggs in an hour.

- [ ] **a.** 25
- [ ] **b.** 50
- [ ] **c.** 75
- [ ] **d.** 100

53. In which classic coming-of-age movie does Daniel Stern utter this line: "Sure miss playing basketball. I got depressed as hell when my athlete's foot and jock itch went away."

- [ ] **a.** *Stand by Me*
- [ ] **b.** *The Last Picture Show*
- [ ] **c.** *American Graffiti*
- [ ] **d.** *Breaking Away*

54. "There's no crying" in what?

- [ ] **a.** Dodgeball
- [ ] **b.** Soccer

☐ **c.** Baseball
☐ **d.** Marriage

55. Fact or Fiction: *Rambo* is the first movie in the Rambo series.

☐ **a.** Fact
☐ **b.** Fiction

56. *The Deer Hunter* may be best remembered for an infamous scene featuring Christopher Walken and _____.

☐ **a.** Russian roulette
☐ **b.** Acid
☐ **c.** Punji sticks
☐ **d.** Vietnamese fighting rats

57. What is "The stuff dreams are made of"?

☐ **a.** *The Maltese Falcon*
☐ **b.** *The Treasure of the Sierra Madre*
☐ **c.** *Jurassic Park*
☐ **d.** *The Pink Panther*

58. Which one of these actors was *not* a member of The Magnificent Seven?

☐ **a.** Yul Brynner
☐ **b.** Charles Bronson
☐ **c.** James Coburn
☐ **d.** Ernest Borgnine

59. What are the Blues Brothers' names?

☐ **a.** Jake and Elwood
☐ **b.** Jack and Reggie
☐ **c.** Lloyd and Harry
☐ **d.** Bert and Ernie

60. In *Stand By Me*, this dog is ordered to "sic balls."

- [ ] **a.** The Beast
- [ ] **b.** Chopper
- [ ] **c.** Hooch
- [ ] **d.** Kong

Top 5 List

Our five favorite car chase movies:	*Ronin*
	The Road Warrior
	To Live and Die in LA
	Smokey and the Bandit
	The Blues Brothers

---

61. In 1995's kinda-cool *Die Hard* rip-off *Sudden Death*, Jean-Claude Van Damme fights terrorists at the NHL home of this team.

- [ ] **a.** The San Jose Sharks
- [ ] **b.** The Montreal Canadians
- [ ] **c.** The Pittsburgh Penguins
- [ ] **d.** The Boston Bruins

62. To go back in time, Doc and Marty's DeLorean must reach this speed.

- [ ] **a.** 88 mph
- [ ] **b.** 121 mph
- [ ] **c.** 100 mph
- [ ] **d.** Infinity to the 10th power

63. Martin Scorsese's *The Last Waltz* documents this band's farewell concert.

- [ ] **a.** The Band
- [ ] **b.** The Rolling Stones

☐ **c.** Pink Floyd
☐ **d.** Dr. John

64. You've seen *Anchorman*, right? Then you know "Brick killed a guy" with this.

☐ **a.** A lamp
☐ **b.** Brass knuckles
☐ **c.** A trident
☐ **d.** A grenade

65. "If it bleeds, we can kill it," is a line from what badass alien flick?

☐ **a.** *Aliens*
☐ **b.** *Starship Troopers*
☐ **c.** *Predator*
☐ **d.** *Tremors*

66. According to Conan, what is best in life?

☐ **a.** "To conquer and pillage; to set fire to the skies and watch red rain fall upon the oceans."
☐ **b.** "To take, take, take—until everything the world has to offer has been swallowed whole."
☐ **c.** "To shatter your enemies and to break their females as if they were nothing more than wild horses."
☐ **d.** "To crush your enemies, to see them driven before you, and to hear the lamentations of their women."

67. Which Paul Newman/Robert Redford team-up came first?

☐ **a.** *Butch Cassidy and the Sundance Kid*
☐ **b.** *The Sting*

68. "Charlie, here comes the deuce. And when you speak of me, speak well." This line comes from which baseball comedy?

- [ ] **a.** *Bull Durham*
- [ ] **b.** *Major League*
- [ ] **c.** *The Sandlot*
- [ ] **d.** *Major League II*

69. "It's a hell of a thing, killing a man. Take away all he's got and all he's ever gonna have." What tough-as-nails Western does this line come from?

- [ ] **a.** *Unforgiven*
- [ ] **b.** *Tombstone*
- [ ] **c.** *Once Upon a Time in the West*
- [ ] **d.** *High Plains Drifter*

70. According to the quote, who is literally "the last guy in the world you want to fuck with"?

- [ ] **a.** James Caan in *Thief*
- [ ] **b.** Clint Eastwood in *Dirty Harry*
- [ ] **c.** Chow Yun Fat in *The Killer*
- [ ] **d.** Jon Voight in *Runaway Train*

71. "You know, most people would kill . . . to be treated like a god, just for a few moments." Which classic underdog movie does this come form?

- [ ] **a.** *Hoosiers*
- [ ] **b.** *The Natural*
- [ ] **c.** *Rudy*
- [ ] **d.** *Any Given Sunday*

72. Asphinctersayswhat?

- [ ] **a.** Huh?
- [ ] **b.** What?

73. In the 1976 thriller *Marathon Man*, Laurence Olivier's evil Nazi Dr. Szell uses what as a method of torture?

☐ **a.** Dental tools
☐ **b.** Pick ax
☐ **c.** Water
☐ **d.** Sack full of wooden knobs

Classic Quote

"You could've robbed banks, sold dope, stole your grandmother's pension check, and none of us would have minded. But shaving points off a football game? Man, that's un-American."

—*THE LONGEST YARD* (THE ORIGINAL, NOT THAT WRETCHED ADAM SANDLER THING)

74. Arnold Schwarzenegger's first feature film appearance was *Hercules in New York*. But, he went by a different last name. What was it?

☐ **a.** Arnold Schwarz
☐ **b.** Arnold Strong
☐ **c.** Arnold Steiner
☐ **d.** Arnold the Giant

75. In what movie do Robert De Niro and Joe Pesci play brothers?

☐ **a.** *Once Upon a Time in America*
☐ **b.** *Goodfellas*
☐ **c.** *Casino*
☐ **d.** *Raging Bull*

76. What are the words Ash screws up in *Army of Darkness*, thus causing an undead army to come to life?

- [ ] **a.** Klaatu . . . barada . . . nikto!
- [ ] **b.** Klado . . . bringo . . . meato!
- [ ] **c.** Klinger . . . basta . . . mincer!
- [ ] **d.** Klavar . . . breako . . . nearem!

77. In *Highlander*, this is the only way to kill an immortal.

- [ ] **a.** Brain destroying
- [ ] **b.** Beheading
- [ ] **c.** Disemboweling
- [ ] **d.** Soul sucking

78. What are De Niro's dying words in *Heat*?

- [ ] **a.** "I told you I'm never going back."
- [ ] **b.** "I was this close. . . ."
- [ ] **c.** "Earn this, James . . . earn it. . . ."
- [ ] **d.** "Rosebud."

79. In *The Pink Panther*, what exactly was the Pink Panther?

- [ ] **a.** A diamond
- [ ] **b.** A password
- [ ] **c.** A girl
- [ ] **d.** A Faberge egg

80. In the Bond flick *Goldfinger*, the villain—y'know, Goldfinger—cheats an opponent at this game.

- [ ] **a.** Rummy
- [ ] **b.** Baccarat
- [ ] **c.** Poker
- [ ] **d.** Mahjong

Did You Know? During WWII, the Oscar statues for the Academy Awards were made of plaster due to a shortage of metal.

81. Who "always leave[s] one bullet, either for myself or for my enemy"?

    ☐ **a.** Bill Paxton in *Aliens*
    ☐ **b.** Chow Yun Fat in *The Killer*
    ☐ **c.** James Caan in *The Killer Elite*
    ☐ **d.** Kurt Russell in *Escape from New York*

82. In *Stripes*, Bill Murray says "Chicks dig [him] because . . ."

    ☐ **a.** He rarely wears underwear
    ☐ **b.** He uses cigarettes as cologne
    ☐ **c.** He wears condoms out on a first date
    ☐ **d.** He can bench-press a Buick

83. What is the name of Judge Smail's super-sexy niece in *Caddyshack*?

    ☐ **a.** Lacey Underall
    ☐ **b.** Flower Never
    ☐ **c.** Ruby Diamond
    ☐ **d.** Jenny Flex

84. In *Reservoir Dogs*, which member of the crew brutally slices off the undercover cop's ear?

    ☐ **a.** Mr. Blue
    ☐ **b.** Mr. Blonde
    ☐ **c.** Mr. Pink
    ☐ **d.** Mr. Orange

85. What is Steven Seagal's job in *Under Siege*?

☐ **a.** Cook
☐ **b.** Stripper
☐ **c.** Helicopter Pilot
☐ **d.** Painter

86. In the film noir classic *Gun Crazy*, the deadly couple go together like:

☐ **a.** Cold and death
☐ **b.** Guns and ammunition
☐ **c.** Peanuts and Payday
☐ **d.** Sex and violence

87. Who played Shaft in the original *Shaft*?

☐ **a.** Richard Roundtree
☐ **b.** Ron O'Neal
☐ **c.** Fred Williamson
☐ **d.** Rudy Ray Moore

88. "Hats for Bats. Keeps bats warm. Gracias." Name the movie.

☐ **a.** *Major League*
☐ **b.** *Rookie of the Year*
☐ **c.** *Bad News Bears*
☐ **d.** *Eight Men Out*

89. What is the name of Dan Aykroyd's auto parts king in *Tommy Boy*?

☐ **a.** Ray Stantz
☐ **a.** Bill Swerski
☐ **b.** Ray Zalinsky
☐ **c.** Harry Sultenfuss

90. This sports star played Roger Murdock, the copilot in *Airplane*.

   ☐ **a.** Bill Walton
   ☐ **b.** Joe Namath
   ☐ **c.** Charles Barkley
   ☐ **d.** Kareem Abdul-Jabbar

91. *Weekend at Bernie's*: it's possibly the best movie ever. What's Bernie's last name?

   ☐ **a.** Moorhead
   ☐ **b.** Lomax
   ☐ **c.** Higeoff
   ☐ **d.** Madoff

92. In *Blazing Saddles*, this character is "only pawn in game of life."

   ☐ **a.** Mongo
   ☐ **b.** Dingo
   ☐ **c.** Ringo
   ☐ **d.** Jango

Classic Quote

"Okay, let me explain something to you. I'm not Mr. Lebowski. You're Mr. Lebowski. I'm the Dude. So that's what you call me. That or His Dudeness ... Duder ... or El Duderino, if, you know, you're not into the whole brevity thing."

—THE DUDE, *THE BIG LEBOWSKI*

93. In *The Jerk*, Steve Martin's Navin Johnson thinks what are defective?

☐ **a.** Gas tanks
☐ **b.** Dogs
☐ **c.** Sandwich wrappers
☐ **d.** Oil cans

94. *Trading Places*, the classic Eddie Murphy/Dan Aykroyd comedy, revolves around a commodities brokerage in Philadelphia. What's the name of the brokerage?

☐ **a.** Foley and Elwood
☐ **b.** Duke and Duke
☐ **c.** Mortimer and Randolph
☐ **d.** Bonnie and Clyde

95. The line, "You work your side of the street and I'll work mine" comes from which Steve McQueen flick?

☐ **a.** *Bullitt*
☐ **b.** *The Getaway*
☐ **c.** *Papillon*
☐ **d.** *The Sand Pebbles*

96. In the action-sci-fi classic *Predator*, Arnold Schwarzenegger goes by what name?

☐ **a.** Wretch
☐ **b.** Hitch
☐ **c.** Butch
☐ **d.** Dutch

97. Conan the Barbarian knows a riddle. What is it?

☐ **a.** The riddle of steel
☐ **b.** The riddle of power

☐ **c.** The riddle of strength
☐ **d.** The riddle of iron

98. "Attica! Attica!" What's the movie?

☐ **a.** *Dog Day Afternoon*
☐ **b.** *Serpico*
☐ **c.** *The Brothers McMullan*
☐ **d.** *Escape from Alcatraz*

99. In the first film in the series, who do the Ghostbusters battle?

☐ **a.** Zule
☐ **b.** The Judge
☐ **c.** Rayal
☐ **d.** The Weaver

100. Match the Bond gadget with the movie it appeared in.

☐ **i.** Lotus Esprit   **a.** *The Spy Who Loved Me*
☐ **ii.** Laser Watch   **b.** *Thunderbolt*
☐ **iii.** Jetpack   **c.** *Goldeneye*
☐ **iv.** Dentonite Toothpaste   **d.** *License to Kill*

ANSWER KEY
CHAPTER 1. THE CINEMA: MEN AT THE MOVIES

1. a.

2. a. And we're endlessly thankful that he switched careers.

3. a.

4. d.

5. c. That's classic pre-*Pirates* Johnny.

6. c.

7. a. Go ahead, make his day.

8. c.

9. d.

10. b.

11. c.

12. a.

13. c.

14. d.

15. d. Contains one of the flat-out best shootouts ever.

16. c.

17. d.

18. a.

19. b.

20. d.

21. a. And we wouldn't expect anything less.

22. a.

23. i. d; ii. a; iii. b; iv. c

24. d.

25. c.

26. a.

27. b.

28. a.

29. d.

30. c.

31. d.

32. d.

33. b.

34. c.

35. b.

36. d.

37. a.

38. a.

39. a.

40. d.

41. b.

42. b. And Lee Van Cleef played "The Bad."

43. i. b; ii. f; iii. e; iv. g; v. c;
    vi. d; vii. a

44. c.

45. d. Louisville Slugger, to be precise.

46. b.

47. a.

48. a.

49. b.

50. a.

51. i. d; ii. a; iii. e; iv. c; v. b

52. b.

53. d.

54. c.

55. b. The first film in the series is *First Blood.*

56. a.

57. a.

58. d. But he was in *The Dirty Dozen.*

59. a.

60. b.

61. c.

62. a.

63. a.

64. c.

65. c.

66. d. Can't say we disagree!

67. a.

68. a.

69. a.

70. a. This is an underviewed gem—Netflix it!

71. a.

72. b.

73. a.

74. b.

75. d.

76. a.

77. b.

78. a.

79. a.

80. a. And it's Bond's intrusion that causes that hot blonde to end up all covered in gold. It was worth it . . .

81. b.

82. a.

83. a.

84. b.

85. a.

86. b.

87. a.

88. a.

89. c.

90. d.

91. b.

92. a.

93. d.

94. b.

95. a.

96. d. Why that is, we have no idea. He certainly doesn't have a Dutch accent.

97. a.

98. a.

99. a.

100. i. a; ii. c; iii. b; iv. d

SCORE!

81–100: Part Clint Eastwood, part Jim Brown, part Burt Reynolds—you're a walking/talking incarnation of guy cinema.

61–80: James Bond level of guyness. Roger Moore James Bond, though—you're no Sean Connery.

41–60: *Terminator 3*. Not good, not bad, 100 percent average. Nothing to be ashamed of.

21–40: That awful remake of *The Bad News Bears*? That's you.

0–20: Please, put the book down, you're ladying it up. I'm pretty sure *Powerpuff Girls* is on.

CHAPTER 2

SPORTS: PLAY BALL

Sports. The manliest of all activities—with the exception of sniper rifle stuff, throat ripping, and juggling hand grenades. The gridiron, the frozen tundra, the walk-off home run, the hockey fight knock out, the soul-shattering slam-dunk—what's not to love? Nothing stirs our emotions like "the thrill of victory . . . the agony of defeat."

Sadly, odds are you're not a professional athlete. So you've got to prove your sporting prowess another way: with *pure testicular knowledge*! It's game time.

1. Everyone loves a good home run. But sometimes hitting a dinger requires crowding the plate, and crowding can lead to the manliest act in baseball: getting drilled by a pitch. The all-time record for getting plunked in a career is 287 times (ouch!) Which hall of famer set the mark?

   ☐ **a.** Frank Robinson
   ☐ **b.** Carlton Fisk
   ☐ **c.** Nap Lajoie
   ☐ **d.** Hughie Jennings

2. It's a rare thing to see a player take home both the MVP and the Cy Young awards in the same year. Rarer still is for that person to go on to win the World Series—it's only happened twice—and both times it happened to the same team. Which team was it?

   ☐ **a.** St. Louis Cardinals
   ☐ **b.** Oakland A's
   ☐ **c.** Detroit Tigers
   ☐ **d.** New York Yankees

Did You Know? The state sport of Maryland is jousting.

---

3. The Cy Young award is given to the best pitcher in each league at the end of the season. You have to be pretty good to have an award named after you, and Cy Young was one of the best. How many wins did Cy pick up in his 22-season career?

   ☐ **a.** 313
   ☐ **b.** 422
   ☐ **c.** 386
   ☐ **d.** 511

4. Considered "The Great One" this man is the only professional athlete to win eight, that's right, *eight*, consecutive MVP awards.

☐ **a.** Michael Jordan
☐ **b.** Wilt Chamberlain
☐ **c.** Babe Ruth
☐ **d.** Wayne Gretzky

5. A game-winning goal in hockey is not necessarily as glorious as it sounds (all it means is that the player scored the deciding goal, even if it's early on in the game). But for the person who scored the goal, it's still pretty nice. Who is the all-time leader in game-winning goals with 118?

☐ **a.** Bobby Hull
☐ **b.** Mario Lemieux
☐ **c.** Wayne Gretzky
☐ **d.** Phil Esposito

6. This NBA legend's famous 100-point game was not shown on TV and there are no highlights!

☐ **a.** Walt Frazier
☐ **b.** Kareem Abdul-Jabbar
☐ **c.** Wilt Chamberlain
☐ **d.** Moses Malone

7. This guy is the only player in the history of baseball to be intentionally walked with the bases loaded (talk about a tough call for the manager). Hint: he's also a famous douche.

☐ **a.** Babe Ruth
☐ **b.** Barry Bonds
☐ **c.** Hank Aaron
☐ **d.** Albert Pujols

8. Guns are cool, but gun safety is important unless you want to end up like this NFL player who shot himself in the leg.

☐ **a.** Adam "Pacman" Jones
☐ **b.** Michael Vick
☐ **c.** Plaxico Burress
☐ **d.** Donte Stallworth

Classic Quote

"Taking the best left-handed pitcher in baseball and converting him into a right fielder is one of the dumbest things I ever heard."

—BASEBALL HALL OF FAMER TRIS SPEAKER, TALKING ABOUT BABE RUTH, IN 1919

9. Okay, we all love some Robert Rodriguez (*Desperado*, *From Dusk Till Dawn*) action-movie-style shootouts. But this NBA player took it a little too far when he was arrested for carrying multiple weapons, including a shotgun in a guitar case, while driving a motorcycle down the highway.

☐ **a.** Ron Artest
☐ **b.** Delonte West
☐ **c.** Rasheed Wallace
☐ **d.** Josh Howard

10. This Yankee great was a pretty private fella, but he earned high marks from every guy around when he landed one of the all-time great beauties, Marilyn Monroe.

☐ **a.** Joe DiMaggio
☐ **b.** Mickey Mantle
☐ **c.** Yogi Berra
☐ **d.** Phil Rizzuto

11. Which of these players was *not* a part of the Philadelphia Flyers' "Legion of Doom" line during the 1990s?

☐ **a.** Mikael Renberg
☐ **b.** Eric Lindros
☐ **c.** John LeClair
☐ **d.** Curtis Leschyshyn

12. Of all the things a guy can do to make a living, driving a car 200 MPH might be the coolest. Which one of these cool dudes holds the record for most NASCAR wins?

☐ **a.** Dale Earnhardt
☐ **b.** Jeff Gordon
☐ **c.** Richard Petty
☐ **d.** Rusty Wallace

True Story

The average life span of a major league baseball is six pitches.

13. A real man knows that it's not always about winning (although that is nice) but about giving everything you have and leaving it all on the field. That sentiment is well known to this man, the first (and only) player to win a Super Bowl MVP while losing the game.

☐ **a.** Chuck Howley
☐ **b.** Bart Starr
☐ **c.** Bruce Smith
☐ **d.** Randy White

14. Which sport has the most ridiculous, out-of-control flopping?

☐ **a.** Basketball
☐ **b.** Soccer

15. It takes a strong leg to be a professional NFL kicker, and Steve O'Neal of the New York Jets certainly had that. In 1969, O'Neal set an NFL record for longest punt. How far did he kick it?

☐ **a.** 77 yards
☐ **b.** 101 yards
☐ **c.** 86 yards
☐ **d.** 98 yards

16. This all-time great is the only NBA player to earn more championship rings than he has fingers to put them on.

☐ **a.** Magic Johnson
☐ **b.** Michael Jordan
☐ **c.** Wayne Gretzky
☐ **d.** Bill Russell

17. Which one of these golf greats never won the PGA Championship?

☐ **a.** Arnold Palmer
☐ **b.** Jack Nicklaus
☐ **c.** Gary Player
☐ **d.** John Daly

18. The 1972 Miami Dolphins was the NFL's first perfect team. They were also the first NFL team to feature two 1,000-yard rushers—running backs Larry Csonka and this player.

☐ **a.** Tony Nathan
☐ **b.** Mercury Morris
☐ **c.** Floyd Little
☐ **d.** David Sims

19. The first World Series MVP award was handed out in 1955. Who went home with it?

☐ **a.** Whitey Ford
☐ **b.** Stan Musial
☐ **c.** Bob Turley
☐ **d.** Johnny Podres

True Story
The first ice hockey pucks were made of frozen cow crap.

20. The signature menu item at most ballparks is the hot dog—twelve inches of naturally encased goodness. However, in Milwaukee, this signature dish is the local favorite.

☐ **a.** Chowder
☐ **b.** Bratwurst
☐ **c.** Wienerschnitzel
☐ **d.** Hamburgers

21. The NBA's Sixth Man Award—given to the league's most valuable bench player—was first awarded during the 1982–1983 season. Who won the award?

☐ **a.** Bobby Jones, Philadelphia 76ers
☐ **b.** Kevin McHale, Boston Celtics
☐ **c.** Ricky Pierce, Milwaukee Bucks
☐ **d.** Roy Tarpley, Dallas Mavericks

22. Reading a baseball scorecard is becoming a lost art. Can you do it? Let's see. If you come across an E5, what does that mean?

☐ **a.** Error, Center Field
☐ **b.** Error, First Base
☐ **c.** Error, Fifth Inning
☐ **d.** Error, Third Base

23. If you want to talk about amazing, improbable feats, you might start the conversation with this: *a walk-off, inside the park, grand slam*. It's only been done once, and it was accomplished by this all-time great.

☐ **a.** Willie Mays
☐ **b.** Rickey Henderson
☐ **c.** Roberto Clemente
☐ **d.** Ernie Banks

24. In football, a 3–4 defense refers to what type of alignment?

☐ **a.** Three linemen and four linebackers
☐ **b.** Three linebackers and four linemen
☐ **c.** Three defensive backs and four linemen
☐ **d.** Three linemen and four defensive backs

Classic Quote
"Nobody in football should be called a genius.
A genius is a guy like Norman Einstein."

—JOE THEISMANN

25. Fact or Fiction: When Ron Artest climbed into the stands and attacked a fan on November 19, 2004 (now known as "the Malice at the Palace"), he became the first professional athlete to physically strike a fan during a game.

☐ **a.** Fact, that's why it was such a big deal
☐ **b.** Fiction

26. The Super Bowl is the most popular thing on TV—that's not exactly news. The 2011 Super Bowl (deciding the champion of the 2010 season) attracted how many viewers?

☐ **a.** 84 million
☐ **b.** 53 million

☐ **c.** 77 million
☐ **d.** 111 million

27. The United States leads the all-time Summer Olympic medals list with a whopping 2,295 medals (that's a thousand more than second place). The United States also has 253 Winter Olympic medals, second only to this country.

☐ **a.** Norway
☐ **b.** Finland
☐ **c.** Sweden
☐ **d.** Germany

28. This man is the all-time hits leader in MLB history with 4,256 hits but he is *not* enshrined in the baseball hall of fame.

☐ **a.** Ty Cobb
☐ **b.** Pete Rose
☐ **c.** Rickey Henderson
☐ **d.** Paul Molitor

29. A helmet-to-helmet hit by this Oakland Raider left New England Patriots wide receiver Darryl Stingley permanently paralyzed.

☐ **a.** Jeff Barnes
☐ **b.** Cliff Branch
☐ **c.** George Buehler
☐ **d.** Jack Tatum

Classic Quote

"We're going to turn this team around 360 degrees."

—JASON KIDD

30. Guys like to watch women's tennis, and we don't think it's any mystery why. But viewers and players alike got more than they bargained for when a fan stabbed this player during a match in 1993.

☐ **a.** Steffi Graf
☐ **b.** Monica Seles
☐ **c.** Katherine Keil
☐ **d.** Gabriela Sabatini

31. The Jack Adams award is given to the NHL coach of the year. Many coaches have won the award twice, but only one coach has taken home the honor three times. Name that coach.

☐ **a.** Don Cherry
☐ **b.** Scotty Bowman
☐ **c.** Jacques Demers
☐ **d.** Pat Burns

32. Javier Sotomayor set the world high jump record in 1992 by jumping this high.

☐ **a.** 6'5"
☐ **b.** 7'2½"
☐ **c.** 8'½"
☐ **d.** 10'3½"

33. As of the 2011 season, there have been 272 no-hitters thrown in baseball history. That amounts to roughly three per year for the last 100 or so years—so yeah, not very many. But in maybe the most improbable two-game stretch ever, this pitcher threw *back-to-back no-hitters*.

☐ **a.** Johnny Vander Meer
☐ **b.** Nolan Ryan
☐ **c.** Cy Young
☐ **d.** Ewell Blackwell

34. The "Iron Man" Cal Ripken Jr. holds the record for most con-
    secutive games played. What number did the streak end at?

    ☐ **a.** 2,632
    ☐ **b.** 3,001
    ☐ **c.** 2,110
    ☐ **d.** 1,998

35. These two men combined to form the only father/son duo to
    hit home runs in the same major league baseball game.

    ☐ **a.** Bobby/Barry Bonds
    ☐ **b.** Ken Jr./Ken Griffey
    ☐ **c.** Felipe/Moises Alou
    ☐ **d.** Cal Ripken/Cal Ripken Jr.

36. Which pitcher holds the record for most strikeouts in a sea-
    son in the modern era with 383?

    ☐ **a.** Sandy Koufax
    ☐ **b.** Randy Johnson
    ☐ **c.** Nolan Ryan
    ☐ **d.** Pedro Martinez

37. In baseball, the Gold Glove Award is given out to the best
    fielder at each position. Lots of players have won multiple
    Gold Gloves, but only one player has won a Gold Glove at
    multiple positions. Who was it?

    ☐ **a.** Roberto Clemente
    ☐ **b.** Darin Erstad
    ☐ **c.** Kevin Youkilis
    ☐ **d.** Robin Ventura

38. The last player to win baseball's Triple Crown (leading the league in HRs, RBIs and AVG.) was Carl Yastrzemski in 1967. Only two players have ever done it twice, and one was Ted Williams. Who was the other?

- ☐ **a.** Ty Cobb
- ☐ **b.** Rogers Hornsby
- ☐ **c.** Lou Gehrig
- ☐ **d.** Frank Robinson

39. This major leaguer has the distinction of playing in more all-star games than any other. He made the trip to the midsummer classic twenty-one times.

- ☐ **a.** Stan Musial
- ☐ **b.** Willie Mays
- ☐ **c.** Carl Yastrzemski
- ☐ **d.** Hank Aaron

40. Who was the first football player to be featured on the cover of the Madden NFL video game?

- ☐ **a.** Steve Young
- ☐ **b.** Emmitt Smith
- ☐ **c.** Eddie George
- ☐ **d.** Marshall Faulk

Did You Know? Before 1900, prizefights lasted up to 100 rounds.

41. Which of the following NBA players was *not* a member of the "Fab Five" at Michigan?

- ☐ **a.** Chris Webber
- ☐ **b.** Jalen Rose
- ☐ **c.** Juwan Howard
- ☐ **d.** Jim Jackson

42. This man has won more NBA MVPs than any other, and he has six trophies to prove it.

   ☐ **a.** Wilt Chamberlain
   ☐ **b.** Michael Jordan
   ☐ **c.** Kareem Abdul-Jabbar
   ☐ **d.** Bill Russell

43. Triple-doubles are not easy to come by, but don't tell this guy: He's the one NBA player who actually averaged a triple-double for an entire season. His final line? 30.8 pts., 12.5 boards, 11.4 assists. Y'know, no big deal.

   ☐ **a.** Michael Jordan
   ☐ **b.** Moses Malone
   ☐ **c.** Oscar Robertson
   ☐ **d.** Magic Johnson

44. The 1971 boxing match dubbed "the Fight of the Century" resulted in the first ever professional loss for Muhammad Ali. It came at the hands of this man.

   ☐ **a.** George Foreman
   ☐ **b.** Joe Frazier
   ☐ **c.** Ken Norton
   ☐ **d.** Sonny Liston

45. Who's responsible for this infamous quote: "My style is impetuous, my defense impregnable and I'm just ferocious. I want your heart. I want to eat your children. Praise be to Allah!"?

   ☐ **a.** Charles Barkley
   ☐ **b.** Mike Tyson
   ☐ **c.** Darryl Strawberry
   ☐ **d.** Lawrence Taylor

46. In maybe the greatest job of drafting by one team in NBA history, the Celtics landed three Hall of Famers in one draft. Which draft was it?

☐ **a.** 1956
☐ **b.** 1962
☐ **c.** 1971
☐ **d.** 1983

47. Fact or Fiction: Dock Ellis once threw a no-hitter while tripping on LSD.

☐ **a.** Fact
☐ **b.** Fiction

48. How many offensive players are there on the field in a football game?

☐ **a.** Nine
☐ **b.** Ten
☐ **c.** Eleven
☐ **d.** Twelve

> **Did You Know?** The most popular sport at nudist colonies is volleyball.

49. This QB's "guarantee" before Super Bowl III is hugely famous, and it helped make the AFL/NFL merger viable.

☐ **a.** Roger Staubach
☐ **b.** Joe Namath

☐ **c.** Bart Starr
☐ **d.** Johnny Unitas

50. This man has eighty-one interceptions—that's more than any other player in the history of the NFL.

☐ **a.** Rod Woodson
☐ **b.** Paul Krause
☐ **c.** Dick "Night Train" Lane
☐ **d.** Deion Sanders

51. Passing for 4,000 yards in a season is impressive indeed, and this guy has done it eleven times in his career—that's five more than the second-place quarterback! Name that QB.

☐ **a.** Dan Marino
☐ **b.** Steve Young
☐ **c.** Peyton Manning
☐ **d.** Brett Favre

52. They say you can't teach speed. So which of these players had the natural-born talent to steal 130 bases in one season?

☐ **a.** Rickey Henderson
☐ **b.** Lou Brock
☐ **c.** Maury Wills
☐ **d.** Ty Cobb

53. Any time a baseball player grabs 100 RBIs in a season, it's considered a good year. So I guess you'd have to call 1930 a *great* year for this player, when he set the all-time single sea-son mark with 191.

☐ **a.** Lou Gehrig
☐ **b.** Jimmy Foxx
☐ **c.** Babe Ruth
☐ **d.** Hack Wilson

54. If there is a runner on third base when a balk occurs, what happens to him?

☐ **a.** He scores
☐ **b.** He must remain at third base
☐ **c.** He must return to second base
☐ **d.** He scores and the inning automatically ends

55. This university is the all-time leader in NCAA Division 1 championships.

☐ **a.** Duke
☐ **b.** North Carolina
☐ **c.** UCLA
☐ **d.** Kentucky

56. In bowling, the alley on the side of the lane is called what?

☐ **a.** Ditch
☐ **b.** High-speed lane
☐ **c.** Gutter
☐ **d.** Trash

57. Which of the following is *not* a professional boxing championship belt?

☐ **a.** WBA
☐ **b.** IBF
☐ **c.** BWA
☐ **d.** WBC

58. This NBA player's return to play in 1996 after retirement made the cover of *Time* magazine.

☐ **a.** Larry Bird
☐ **b.** Magic Johnson
☐ **c.** Michael Jordan
☐ **d.** Dominique Wilkins

59. Basketball positions are often referred to as numbers. Match the number with the correct position.

i. Shooting guard	**a.** 1
ii. Point guard	**b.** 2
iii. Center	**c.** 3
iv. Power forward	**d.** 4
v. Small forward	**e.** 5

True Story
In 1942, the Boston College Eagles lost their final game of the season to Holy Cross 55–12. The team decided to cancel the celebration they had planned at the Coconut Grove. That night the Coconut Grove burned down, killing 491 people.

60. This NFL franchise used to be known as the Houston Oilers.

☐ **a.** Houston Texans
☐ **b.** Baltimore Ravens
☐ **c.** Tennessee Titans
☐ **d.** Carolina Panthers

61. This NFL stadium is often referred to as "the frozen tundra."

☐ **a.** Giants Stadium
☐ **b.** Lambeau Field
☐ **c.** Soldier Field
☐ **d.** Ralph Wilson Stadium

62. Coach Mike Ditka is about as well known a football name as there is. Which position did he play while in the NFL?

☐ **a.** Linebacker
☐ **b.** Defensive end
☐ **c.** Quarterback
☐ **d.** Tight end

63. The first Super Bowl was played on January 15th, 1967. Who won the game?

☐ **a.** Green Bay Packers
☐ **b.** Kansas City Chiefs
☐ **c.** Baltimore Colts
☐ **d.** Dallas Cowboys

64. How many no-hitters did Nolan Ryan throw?

☐ **a.** Three
☐ **b.** Five
☐ **c.** Seven
☐ **d.** Nine

65. "Shoeless" Joe Jackson and seven other members of the White Sox were implicated in fixing the 1919 World Series, resulting in a win for what team?

☐ **a.** Cincinnati Reds
☐ **b.** St. Louis Cardinals
☐ **c.** Pittsburgh Pirates
☐ **d.** Chicago Cubs

66. Which of these movies tells the story of the 1919 World Series?

☐ **a.** *Bang the Drum Slowly*
☐ **b.** *Eight Men Out*
☐ **c.** *The Natural*
☐ **d.** *Bull Durham*

Classic Quote

"I dunno. I never smoked any Astroturf."

—PITCHER TUG MCGRAW, WHEN ASKED
IF HE PREFERRED TURF TO GRASS

67. French Lick, Indiana, is the hometown of what basketball legend?

☐ **a.** Larry Bird
☐ **b.** John Stockton
☐ **c.** "Pistol" Pete Maravich
☐ **d.** Magic Johnson

68. Match the baseball legend to his team.

☐ **i.** George Brett   **a.** Pirates
☐ **ii.** Mike Schmidt   **b.** Dodgers
☐ **iii.** Sandy Koufax   **c.** Royals
☐ **iv.** Bob Gibson   **d.** Phillies
☐ **v.** Honus Wagner   **e.** Cardinals

69. This southpaw was sometimes referred to as "The left arm of God."

☐ **a.** Whitey Ford
☐ **b.** Lefty Grove
☐ **c.** Warren Spahn
☐ **d.** Sandy Koufax

Classic Quote

"Because there are no fours."

—ANTOINE WALKER WHEN ASKED WHY HE SHOOTS SO MANY
DAMN THREES

70. World Series championship rings are tough to come by, but this beloved Yankee has ten of them.

☐ **a.** Derek Jeter
☐ **b.** Yogi Berra
☐ **c.** Joe DiMaggio
☐ **d.** Babe Ruth

71. Fact or Fiction: Tug-of-war was an Olympic event during the early twentieth century.

☐ **a.** Fact
☐ **b.** Fiction

72. In bowling, what is known as a "turkey"?

☐ **a.** Two gutter balls
☐ **b.** Three consecutive strikes
☐ **c.** Picking up a 7–10 split
☐ **d.** A perfect game

73. What score constitutes a perfect game in bowling?

☐ **a.** 100
☐ **b.** 200
☐ **c.** 300
☐ **d.** 400

74. Fact or Fiction: When basketball players dunk they can stay in the air for over two seconds.

☐ **a.** Fact
☐ **b.** Fiction

75. Who was the first player in NBA history to miss 5,000 free throws?

☐ **a.** Shaquille O'Neal
☐ **b.** Wilt Chamberlain

☐ **c.** Ben Wallace
☐ **d.** Chris Dudley

True Story
Chad Ochocinco once beat a horse in a footrace.

76. In a race, the favored horse wins about what percent of the time?

☐ **a.** 22 percent
☐ **b.** 33 percent
☐ **c.** 44 percent
☐ **d.** 55 percent

77. During WWII, the Pittsburgh Steelers and Philadelphia Eagles were forced to combine teams due to lack of players. What was the name of their new, temporary team?

☐ **a.** The Steel Eagles
☐ **b.** The Steagles
☐ **c.** The Eagleers
☐ **d.** Pittsadelphia Football Co.

78. In golf, what does the term "birdie" refer to?

☐ **a.** Two strokes under par
☐ **b.** One stroke over par
☐ **c.** One stroke under par
☐ **d.** Two strokes over par

79. This golf legend is sometimes referred to as "The Golden Bear."

☐ **a.** Jack Nicklaus
☐ **b.** Arnold Palmer
☐ **c.** Ben Hogan
☐ **d.** Tom Watson

80. The Montreal Canadiens hold the record for the most Stanley Cup Championships. How many do they have?

☐ **a.** Eleven
☐ **b.** Eighteen
☐ **c.** Twenty-four
☐ **d.** Thirty

81. The MLB record for most victories by a coach is 3,755. It's held by this skipper.

☐ **a.** Connie Mack
☐ **b.** Tony LaRussa
☐ **c.** Tommy Lasorda
☐ **d.** Sparky Anderson

True Story
Hulk Hogan was the first wrestler to make the cover of *Sports Illustrated*.

82. The first World Series was played between the Boston Red Sox and the Pittsburgh Pirates in 1903. It was a best of how many series?

☐ **a.** Five
☐ **b.** Seven
☐ **c.** Nine
☐ **d.** Twelve

83. The first Kentucky Derby took place in what year?

☐ **a.** 1850
☐ **b.** 1875
☐ **c.** 1900
☐ **d.** 1925

84. Which of these teams was *not* a member of the ABA?

☐ **a.** San Antonio Spurs
☐ **b.** Indiana Pacers
☐ **c.** Golden State Warriors
☐ **d.** Denver Nuggets

85. In what year did the NBA institute the three-point line?

☐ **a.** 1972–1973
☐ **b.** 1979–1980
☐ **c.** 1985–1986
☐ **d.** 1990–1991

86. NFL rushing legend turned actor, Jim Brown led the league in rushing how many times?

☐ **a.** Four
☐ **b.** Six
☐ **c.** Eight
☐ **d.** Ten

87. It's simply known as "the catch." Say it and most any NFL fan will immediately know what you're talking about. So . . . which NFL player made "the catch"?

☐ **a.** Jerry Rice
☐ **b.** Chris Carter
☐ **c.** Irving Fryar
☐ **d.** Dwight Clark

88. This boxer is the only heavyweight champion to retire with a perfect undefeated record of 49–0.

☐ **a.** Muhammad Ali
☐ **b.** Rocky Marciano
☐ **c.** Mike Tyson
☐ **d.** Sonny Liston

89. "The Giants win the pennant! The Giants win the pennant!" was the call when Bobby Thompson made the "shot heard round the world." Which announcer made the famous call?

☐ **a.** Howard Cosell
☐ **b.** Mel Allen
☐ **c.** Russ Hodges
☐ **d.** Bob Prince

90. A football game between these heated rivals featured one of the most bizarre endings in history. It ended on a last-second kickoff return while the band was rushing the field to celebrate.

☐ **a.** Cal and Stanford
☐ **b.** Miami and Florida State
☐ **c.** Oklahoma and Texas
☐ **d.** BC and Notre Dame

91. Why did the owners of the Red Sox sell Babe Ruth to the Yankees for $100,000?

☐ **a.** They didn't think he had the talent to succeed in the league.
☐ **b.** They were worried about his drinking.
☐ **c.** The Babe was unhappy with the direction of the team and demanded a trade.
☐ **d.** They needed money to finance their Broadway play.

92. This golfer was the youngest ever to win a Masters.

☐ **a.** Arnold Palmer
☐ **b.** Tiger Woods
☐ **c.** Jack Nicklaus
☐ **d.** Tom Watson

93. In a move that would forever change the game of baseball, free agency was enacted in this year.

- ☐ **a.** 1970
- ☐ **b.** 1975
- ☐ **c.** 1980
- ☐ **d.** 1985

Classic Quote

"If you've only got a day to live, come see the Toronto Maple Leafs. It'll seem like forever."

—CHICAGO BLACKHAWK'S PLAY-BY-PLAY ANNOUNCER PAT FOLEY

94. The historic line "Win one for the Gipper" was spoken in a halftime speech by what coach?

- ☐ **a.** Joe Paterno
- ☐ **b.** Paul Bryant
- ☐ **c.** Knute Rockne
- ☐ **d.** Glenn Scobey Warner

95. When you hear the name Jim Thorpe, you probably think great athlete. And that's true. How many events did he actually win during the 1912 Olympics?

- ☐ **a.** Six
- ☐ **b.** Eight
- ☐ **c.** Ten
- ☐ **d.** Twelve

96. Fact or Fiction: The "Immaculate Reception" occurred in the Super Bowl.

- ☐ **a.** Fact
- ☐ **b.** Fiction

97. Perfect games are just about the rarest thing in baseball. Only thing that could make them more exciting? Throwing one in the World Series. And this man did it.

☐ **a.** Bob Gibson
☐ **b.** Goose Gossage
☐ **c.** Don Larsen
☐ **d.** Steve Carlton

98. Which New York Met hit the ball that rolled through Bill Buckner's legs in game 6 of the 1986 World Series—a game that the Red Sox eventually lost (along with the series).

☐ **a.** Keith Hernandez
☐ **b.** Mookie Wilson
☐ **c.** Lenny Dykstra
☐ **d.** Darryl Strawberry

99. Which of these thoroughbreds is *not* a Triple Crown winner?

☐ **a.** War Admiral
☐ **b.** Man o' War
☐ **c.** Gallant Fox
☐ **d.** Seattle Slew

100. For horses to compete in the Triple Crown of thoroughbred racing, they must be this old.

☐ **a.** Two
☐ **b.** Three
☐ **c.** Four
☐ **d.** Five

ANSWER KEY
CHAPTER 2. SPORTS: PLAY BALL

1. d. Craig Biggio holds the modern record.

2. c.

3. d.

4. d. That might have something to do with him earning the nickname "The Great One."

5. d.

6. c.

7. b.

8. c.

9. b.

10. a.

11. d.

12. c.

13. a.

14. b.

15. d.

16. d. Unless, between now and this book's publication, Michael Jordan gets in a horrific lawn mowing accident and loses five fingers.

17. a.

18. b.

19. d.

20. b.

21. a.

22. d.

23. c.

24. a.

25. b.

26. d.

27. a.

28. b.

29. d.

30. b.

31. d.

32. c.

33. a.

34. a.

35. b.

36. c.

37. b.

38. b.

39. d.

40. c.

41. d.

42. c.

43. c.

44. b. The first of three fights against Frazier. Ali won the final two.

45. b.

46. a.

47. a.

48. c. Five offensive linemen, one quarterback, one or two running backs, one tight end, and two or three wide receivers in a basic alignment.

49. b. It's the thing "Broadway Joe" is most famous for.

50. b.

51. c.

52. a. And he did it in 149 games. Someone get this guy a Gatorade.

53. d. That's right; he had 191 RBIs in 1930.The closest anyone has been in over seventy years is Manny Ramirez in 1999 with 165. This one will probably be around a while.

54. a.

55. c. "The Legend" John Wooden helped this happen when he took ten of twelve titles between 1964 and 1975.

56. c.

57. c.

58. b. Magic returned to the NBA after being diagnosed with the HIV virus, and not surprisingly, it was big news.

59. i. a; ii. b; iii. e; iv. d; v. c

60. c. They moved east in 1997.

61. b. Surprise: it gets a little cold in Green Bay during the winter.

62. d. Ditka was the first tight end ever elected to the NFL Hall of Fame.

63. a. The Packers, led by quarterback Bart Starr, took home the first two Super Bowl trophies.

64. c. Two in '72, one in '74, one in'75, one in '80, one in '90, and his final one in '91.

65. a.

66. b. This John Cusack classic told the story of the "Chicago Black Sox" scandal.

67. a. He is sometimes referred to as "the hick from French Lick."

68. i. c; ii. d; iii. b; iv. e; v. a

69. d. In the '65 season Koufax had a 26-8 record with a 2.04 ERA, a .855 WHIP, and 382 strikeouts in 335.2 innings. Just . . . just . . . *damn*.

70. b. 10 Rings from the guy who gave us "The future ain't what is used to be" and "You can observe a lot by watching."

71. a. Brings back memories of middle school gym class.

72. b.

73. c. There are ten frames, and a strike on every frame gives thirty pins (or points) per frame.

74. b. It's nearly impossible to get off the ground for even one second flat. That would require a vertical jump of over 4'.

75. b.

76. b.

77. b.

78. c. Now if only we could get more of these.

79. a.

80. c. Don't go around thinking their fans are satisfied though.

81. a.

82. c. The Red Sox won the series five games to three.

83. b. And it was won by a horse named Aristides.

84. c. The Warriors started in Philadelphia in 1946.

85. b.

86. c. Which is really, really ridiculous considered he only played in the NFL for nine years—and retired when he was still healthy!

87. d.

88. b. He also had a *ridiculous* knockout rate of 87.8 percent.

89. c.

90. a.

91. a. Took Boston fans a little while to get over this one. "A little while" meaning never.

92. b.

93. b. Whether it was for the better is for you to decide, but it's not going anywhere, that's for sure.

94. c. The Gipper was a former player, and was played in the film *Knute Rockne: All American* by Ronald Reagan.

95. b. Oh, by the way, he also played professional baseball and football.

96. b. Many people think so, but it actually occurred in the divisional playoff round.

97. c.

98. b.

99. b.

100. b.

SCORE!

81–100: If Gretzky and Jordan ever had a baby, and we later found out that Jordan's dad was Bill Russell, you would be the result.

61–80: What's up Steve Young? You are classy and efficient, you don't have the rings of Montana, but you know you played well, and you do have some jewelry to boot.

41–60: You're kinda like Vin Baker. Lots of talent, but all the potential washed away.

21–40: Get the cream, the clear, some greenies, or just anything to enhance *that* performance.

0–20: Hey, Buckner, get off the field!

CHAPTER 3

RATIONS: HOT DOGS, BEER, AND MORE

We think Homer Simpson said it best: "All normal people love meat. If I went to a barbecue and there was no meat, I would say 'Yo, Goober! Where's the meat!?' I'm trying to impress people here, Lisa. You don't win friends with salad."

That's the guy relationship with food: it's BBQ, meat, beers . . . powerful sustenance. It's guys standing around the grill, arguing BBQ techniques, complaining about their wives. And now that it's quiz time, let's see if you can cut the mustard . . . .

1. What is the bestselling condiment in the United States?

   ☐ **a.** Salsa
   ☐ **b.** Mayo
   ☐ **c.** Ketchup
   ☐ **d.** Mustard

2. It's Sunday BBQ time. You're working on some pork chops and you know your buddies will kill you if they're overcooked. So . . . what temperature should the pork be cooked to?

   ☐ **a.** 95°F
   ☐ **b.** 125°F
   ☐ **c.** 160°F
   ☐ **d.** 200°F

3. Bonus BBQ question: When you're planning a big grill session, how much meat should you plan for each person? On average, of course—we have no idea how fat your pals are.

   ☐ **a.** ½ pound
   ☐ **b.** 1 pound
   ☐ **c.** 1½ pounds
   ☐ **d.** 2 pounds

4. Linguica is a popular sausage from which country?

   ☐ **a.** Italy
   ☐ **b.** Portugal
   ☐ **c.** Spain
   ☐ **d.** Sweden

5. Some people keep tarantulas as pets, but in this country you can find them on the menu.

   ☐ **a.** Cambodia
   ☐ **b.** France

☐ **c.** Australia
☐ **d.** Japan

6. Everyone knows the term "ice-cold beer," but the truth is different beers have different ideal serving temperatures. With that in mind, what is the suggested temperature to throw back a nice dark beer?

☐ **a.** 40–45°F
☐ **b.** 45–50°F
☐ **c.** 50–55°F
☐ **d.** Room temperature (60°F)

7. What European country is known for drinking beer warm?

☐ **a.** England
☐ **b.** France
☐ **c.** Germany
☐ **d.** Belgium

8. Budweiser uses a horse as its logo—most everyone knows that. But do you know the breed of horse?

☐ **a.** Lokai
☐ **b.** Clydesdale
☐ **c.** Mustang
☐ **d.** Appaloosa

Did You Know? The word *honeymoon* is said to have come from the ancient Babylon tradition of honey month where, for a month after the wedding, the father of the bride would provide his new son-in-law with all the mead (honey alcohol) he could toss back.

---

9. Lots of guys enjoy a brew or two (or five) when they go to a ballgame. What is the standard cutoff point for serving in most major league parks?

☐ **a.** Fifth inning
☐ **b.** Seventh inning
☐ **c.** Ninth inning
☐ **d.** Trick question—beer has been outlawed in all U.S. ballparks

10. A Reuben (corned beef, sauerkraut, Swiss cheese, and Russian dressing) is typically served on which type of bread?

☐ **a.** Marble
☐ **b.** Whole wheat
☐ **c.** Rye
☐ **d.** Pumpernickel

11. When preparing a meal, which of these meats should *not* be marinated for a long time (usually just thirty minutes or less).

☐ **a.** Fish
☐ **b.** Pork
☐ **c.** Beef
☐ **d.** Chicken

12. This alcohol is the only liquid the body can consume as food for upwards of thirty days without shutting down.

☐ **a.** Vodka
☐ **b.** Beer
☐ **c.** Wine
☐ **d.** Whiskey

13. Typical American bacon (mmm . . . bacon) comes from what part of the pig?

☐ **a.** Back
☐ **b.** Loin
☐ **c.** Belly
☐ **d.** Breast

14. The natural casing on a typical Italian sausage is made out of what unappetizing organ?

☐ **a.** Intestines
☐ **b.** Skin
☐ **c.** Stomach
☐ **d.** Heart

15. A porterhouse steak—also known as a T-Bone, features a T-shaped bone with meat on each side. When separated, those two cuts of meat have their own names. What are they?

☐ **a.** Strip steak and tenderloin steak
☐ **b.** Hanger steak and flank steak
☐ **c.** Rib-eye steak and cube steak
☐ **d.** Round steak and sirloin steak

16. Fact or Fiction: It's been confirmed that the number "33" on the Rolling Rock bottle represents the thirty-three words in the brewing pledge written on the back of the bottle.

☐ **a.** Fact
☐ **b.** Fiction

True Story
Baseball fans consume an average of 26 million hot dogs at U.S. baseball stadiums each year.

17. Match the brand with the style of beer:

☐ **i.** Guinness   **a.** Pilsner
☐ **ii.** Killian's Irish Red   **b.** Lager
☐ **iii.** New Castle Brown   **c.** Stout
☐ **iv.** Heineken   **d.** Dark Lager
☐ **v.** St. Pauli Girl   **e.** Brown Ale

18. In order for an alcohol to be considered tequila, it has to be made with at least 51 percent of this product:

☐ **a.** Blue agave
☐ **b.** Coconut
☐ **c.** Sugar cane
☐ **d.** Pine sap

19. "Have it your way" is the slogan of what fast food restaurant?

☐ **a.** McDonald's
☐ **b.** Wendy's
☐ **c.** Burger King
☐ **d.** Arby's

20. What hot dog brand is the sponsor for the annual hot dog eating contest held at Coney Island?

☐ **a.** Nathan's World Famous
☐ **b.** Hebrew National
☐ **c.** Ball Park
☐ **d.** Oscar Mayer

21. The more you work out, the more calories you need to sustain your energy. How many calories does Olympic swimmer Michael Phelps eat during training?

☐ **a.** 2,000 calories
☐ **b.** 3,000 calories

- [ ] **c.** 12,000 calories
- [ ] **d.** 15,000 calories

22. "What are you eating today?" Name the chain.

- [ ] **a.** Sonic
- [ ] **b.** P.F. Chang's
- [ ] **c.** White Castle
- [ ] **d.** Arby's

23. Most people think of a tiny little tin can when they hear the word tuna but the real fish is much, *much* bigger than that. On average, how big is an adult bluefin tuna?

- [ ] **a.** 125 pounds
- [ ] **b.** 330 pounds
- [ ] **c.** 550 pounds
- [ ] **d.** 710 pounds

True Story
In Germany you can purchase beer-flavored Popsicles.

24. Fact or Fiction: The deep-dish pizza was invented in Chicago.

- [ ] **a.** Fact
- [ ] **b.** Fiction

25. Serious Philly cheesesteak fans often prefer this cheese. It's even recommended by the owner of a famous cheesesteak joint, Geno's in Philadelphia.

- [ ] **a.** American
- [ ] **b.** Swiss
- [ ] **c.** Provolone
- [ ] **d.** Cheese Whiz

26. A delicious meal, this sandwich is made with French toast, turkey, ham, and butter. Also, you better have it with a side of jelly (or syrup . . . yum).

☐ **a.** Monte Cristo
☐ **b.** Rachel
☐ **c.** Reuben
☐ **d.** Chip Buddy

27. What is done to beef in order to make it corned beef?

☐ **a.** Boiled with corn
☐ **b.** Cured in salt brine, then simmered
☐ **c.** Cured in salt brine, then smoked
☐ **d.** Smoked and boiled

28. With few exceptions, beer has a shelf life before it becomes stale. For most beers that shelf life is roughly how long?

☐ **a.** One month
☐ **b.** Four months
☐ **c.** Nine months
☐ **d.** One year

29. Red meat is awesome. It's basically the king of all foods. How much red meat does the average American consume per year?

☐ **a.** 35 pounds
☐ **b.** 60 pounds
☐ **c.** 110 pounds
☐ **d.** 220 pounds

True Story
McDonald's is Brazil's largest employer.

30. Mom always said "eat your vegetables." We're not sure why, because by and large, vegetables suck. But some people listen to Mom. How many pounds of vegetables do Americans eat on average every year?

☐ **a.** 64 pounds
☐ **b.** 180 pounds
☐ **c.** 302 pounds
☐ **d.** 415 pounds

31. The average American eats roughly how many calories a day?

☐ **a.** 1,100
☐ **b.** 1,900
☐ **c.** 2,700
☐ **d.** 3,000

32. This fast-food chain founder was known for starring in his own commercials.

☐ **a.** Paul Newton
☐ **b.** Ben Murphy
☐ **c.** Dave Thomas
☐ **d.** Steve Thompson

True Story
Legend has it that the first saucer champagne glass (y'know, the shallow, big-bowled, stemmed glass that fancy people drink out of) was modeled using wax molds of Marie Antoinette's breasts.

33. Fact or Fiction: Chocolate chip cookies were invented by accident when Ruth Wakefield ran out of baker's chocolate and used chunks of semisweet chocolate instead.

☐ **a.** Fact
☐ **b.** Fiction

34. Most guys enjoy a nice, big, meaty hot dog—but maybe not *this* big. What's the weight of the largest commercially available hot dog?

☐ **a.** 2 pounds
☐ **b.** 3 pounds
☐ **c.** 5 pounds
☐ **d.** 7 pounds

35. Name the sandwich: two all-beef patties, special sauce, lettuce, cheese, pickles, onions on a sesame seed bun.

☐ **a.** Whopper
☐ **b.** Big Mac
☐ **c.** Double Double
☐ **d.** Double Quarter Pounder

36. Coffee is the most popular drink in America. How many cups of coffee do Americans consume every day?

☐ **a.** 100 million
☐ **b.** 225 million
☐ **c.** 450 million
☐ **d.** 875 million

37. "Better ingredients, better pizza." You've heard the slogan, now tell us what pizza chain it applies to:

☐ **a.** Pizza Hut
☐ **b.** Domino's
☐ **c.** Papa John's
☐ **d.** Tombstone

38. Burger King goes by a different name in Australia. What is it?

☐ **a.** Burger Lieutenant
☐ **b.** Hungry Jack's

☐ **c.** Royal with Cheese
☐ **d.** Whoppers

39. All right, you're looking down at the dishes, staring at a dirty Teflon pan. If you ruin another one of these things, your wife is going to kill you. So . . . what's the best way to clean it?

☐ **a.** Steel wool sponge and a little vinegar
☐ **b.** Hot, soapy water and a soft sponge
☐ **c.** Dishwasher
☐ **d.** Sprinkle with salt and wipe clean

40. What is the official booze of the United States?

☐ **a.** Bourbon
☐ **b.** Pale ale
☐ **c.** Rye
☐ **d.** Scotch

41. Alcohol does this to your body temperature:

☐ **a.** Makes it rise
☐ **b.** Has no effect
☐ **c.** Depends on how much you drink
☐ **d.** Makes it fall

42. If you take a vodka martini and add this ingredient, it becomes a Gibson.

☐ **a.** Pepper
☐ **b.** Onion
☐ **c.** Sugar cube
☐ **d.** Lemon

True Story
As far as the Lepcha people of Tibet are concerned, the only proper form of payment for a teacher is alcohol.

43. Fact or Fiction: Sucking on a penny can help to beat a Breathalyzer test.

☐ **a.** Fact
☐ **b.** Fiction

> **True Story**
> Years ago in England they would build whistles into beer mugs so drinkers could easily call for another brew. Hence the term "wet my whistle."

44. When talking steaks, what does the term "marbling" refer to?

☐ **a.** Level of marrow in the bones
☐ **b.** Bone content of the meat
☐ **c.** The amount of intramuscular fat
☐ **d.** Salt quantity in the meat

45. What was the first American beer sold in Germany?

☐ **a.** Budweiser
☐ **b.** Yuengling
☐ **c.** Samuel Adams
☐ **d.** Pabst Blue Ribbon

46. This popular drink was used on NASA missions to space, in an effort to make the water taste better.

☐ **a.** Tang
☐ **b.** Kool-Aid
☐ **c.** Gatorade
☐ **d.** Nestle Quick

47. What sandwich shop originally went by the name "Pete's Super Submarines"?

☐ **a.** Arby's
☐ **b.** Quiznos

☐ **c.** Subway
☐ **d.** Carl's Jr.

48. Which major fast food chain was the first to add a value menu?

☐ **a.** McDonald's
☐ **b.** Burger King
☐ **c.** Taco Bell
☐ **d.** Wendy's

49. People have been grilling since the beginning of recorded history, but surprisingly it didn't become a popular American pastime until this decade:

☐ **a.** 1930s
☐ **b.** 1940s
☐ **c.** 1950s
☐ **d.** 1960s

50. What Rat Pack member is responsible for this classic drinking quote? "I feel sorry for people who don't drink. When they wake up in the morning, that's as good as they're going to feel all day."

☐ **a.** Frank Sinatra
☐ **b.** Dean Martin
☐ **c.** Sammy Davis Jr.
☐ **d.** Joey Bishop

51. What rocker gave us this quote? "Vegetarians are cool. All I eat are vegetarians—except for the occasional mountain lion steak."

☐ **a.** Jimmy Buffett
☐ **b.** Kid Rock
☐ **c.** Ted Nugent
☐ **d.** Frank Zappa

52. What exactly is a classic Coney Island hot dog?

☐ **a.** Beef hot dog topped with all-meat chili, chopped white onions, and mustard
☐ **b.** Pork hot dog topped with sauerkraut, ground beef, and secret special sauce
☐ **c.** Beef hot dog topped with diced onions, sliced tomatoes, relish, and a dill pickle spear
☐ **d.** Pork hot dog topped with cream cheese and grilled onions

Did You Know? Many credit Louis Lassen of Louis' Lunch, a lunch wagon in New Haven, Connecticut for selling the first hamburger in 1895.

53. This product is "mmm mmm good!"

☐ **a.** Snickers
☐ **b.** Campbell's Soup
☐ **c.** Easy Mac
☐ **d.** Doritos

54. Like BBQ? Then you would have loved Big Bill, the heaviest pig in history. This porker weighed roughly how many pounds?

☐ **a.** 1,272 pounds
☐ **b.** 1,633 pounds
☐ **c.** 1,985 pounds
☐ **d.** 2,552 pounds

55. Which of the following is not an ingredient in a traditional Bloody Mary?

☐ **a.** Pepper
☐ **b.** Tabasco sauce

☐ **c.** Horseradish
☐ **d.** Carrot juice

56. What is the number one–selling candy in the world?

☐ **a.** Snickers
☐ **b.** Cadbury Dairy Milk
☐ **c.** M&Ms
☐ **d.** Skittles

Classic Quote

"I drink too much. The last time I gave a urine sample it had an olive in it."

—RODNEY DANGERFIELD

57. Believe it or not, researchers have done tests and have concluded that on average it takes this many licks to get to the center of a Tootsie Pop.

☐ **a.** 50
☐ **b.** 150
☐ **c.** 250
☐ **d.** 350

True Story
Tang, Pop Rocks, Cool Whip, and quick-setting Jell-O were all invented by the same man.

58. This city is proud to call itself the Barbecue Capital of the World.

☐ **a.** Lexington, North Carolina
☐ **b.** Houston, Texas
☐ **c.** Nashville, Tennessee
☐ **d.** St. Louis, Missouri

59. Which was not an original Life Savers flavor?

☐ **a.** Cherry
☐ **b.** Lime
☐ **c.** Grape
☐ **d.** Orange

60. Sour Patch Kids originally had this name.

☐ **a.** Mars Men
☐ **b.** Baby Sours
☐ **c.** Sour Chews
☐ **d.** Space Scouts

61. This chocolate maker is also the number one maker of non-chocolate candy.

☐ **a.** M&M Mars
☐ **b.** Hershey's
☐ **c.** Nestle
☐ **d.** Kraft

62. "Taste the Rainbow." You know the line—what candy does it refer to?

☐ **a.** Now and Later
☐ **b.** Starburst
☐ **c.** Skittles
☐ **d.** Life Savers

63. Pabst Blue Ribbon was the first beer to be sold in six packs. Why did PBR choose to sell their beer in packages of six?

☐ **a.** More cost effective to manufacture
☐ **b.** Studies determined that six cans was the first perfect carrying weight for housewives
☐ **c.** At the time, it fit easily in deli coolers
☐ **d.** For ease of stacking

64. Neil Patrick Harris was in a movie involving this fast food chain.

- ☐ **a.** Burger King
- ☐ **b.** White Castle
- ☐ **c.** Sonic
- ☐ **d.** Jack in the Box

65. This U.S. city is considered the "Bratwurst Capital of America."

- ☐ **a.** Reading, Massachusetts
- ☐ **b.** Sheboygan, Wisconsin
- ☐ **c.** Gradwohl, Illinois
- ☐ **d.** Tucker, Kansas

Did You Know? Life Savers spark when you eat them—if you eat them in the dark, you can see the sparks!

---

66. Believe it or not, there is a competitive eating record for cow brains. Superhuman competitive eater Kobayashi holds the record for most cow brains eaten in 15 minutes. How much cow brain did he manage to get down his gullet?

- ☐ **a.** 6.9 pounds
- ☐ **b.** 9.8 pounds
- ☐ **c.** 13.2 pounds
- ☐ **d.** 17.7 pounds

67. The amount spent on fast food by consumers in 1973 was $3 billion. Today it is over:

- ☐ **a.** $25 billion
- ☐ **b.** $80 billion
- ☐ **c.** $110 billion
- ☐ **d.** $300 billion

68. This is the bestselling beer in the United States.

    ☐ **a.** Bud Light
    ☐ **b.** Corona Extra
    ☐ **c.** Budweiser
    ☐ **d.** Miller Lite

69. In diner lingo, what food does "Adam & Eve on a log" refer to?

    ☐ **a.** Two hamburgers with onions and tomato
    ☐ **b.** Two poached eggs with link sausage
    ☐ **c.** Banana split
    ☐ **d.** Hot dog with onions and pickles

70. This fictional character uses spinach to become strong and fight the bad guys.

    ☐ **a.** Batman
    ☐ **b.** Popeye
    ☐ **c.** Captain Planet
    ☐ **d.** The Jolly Green Giant

71. Kielbasa is a traditional sausage from what country?

    ☐ **a.** Poland
    ☐ **b.** Australia
    ☐ **c.** England
    ☐ **d.** Greece

72. Which fast food joint was started by the Raffel Brothers?

☐ **a.** Burger King
☐ **b.** Sonic
☐ **c.** Arby's
☐ **d.** White Castle

73. In this country, McDonald's doesn't serve hamburgers.

☐ **a.** Israel
☐ **b.** China
☐ **c.** India
☐ **d.** Japan

True Story
The longest bar in the world is located at the New Bulldog in Rock Island, Illinois—it's 684 feet long.

74. There is evidence that this may be the only food that does not spoil.

☐ **a.** Honey
☐ **b.** Peanut butter
☐ **c.** Cinnamon
☐ **d.** Mayo

75. This veggie has pretty much zero nutritional value.

☐ **a.** Onion
☐ **b.** Iceberg lettuce
☐ **c.** Potato
☐ **d.** Celery

True Story
You can grab McNuggets on the slopes in Sweden at a "ski-through" McDonald's.

76. McDonald's infamous McRib sandwich debuted in what year?

☐ **a.** 1967
☐ **b.** 1975
☐ **c.** 1981
☐ **d.** 1990

77. Because of the lack of an 'R' sound in the Japanese language, Ronald McDonald goes by what name there?

☐ **a.** Bob McDonald
☐ **b.** Happy Clown
☐ **c.** Donald McDonald
☐ **d.** Silly Clown

78. What was the first pizza chain?

☐ **a.** Domino's
☐ **b.** Papa John's
☐ **c.** Little Caesars
☐ **d.** Pizza Hut

79. Which of these is *not* a real Lucky Charm marshmallow?

☐ **a.** Shooting star
☐ **b.** Rainbow
☐ **c.** Hourglass
☐ **d.** Sun

80. The Flintstones can be seen on the box of what popular cereal?

☐ **a.** Fruity Pebbles
☐ **b.** Cocoa Puffs
☐ **c.** Cookie Crisp
☐ **d.** Corn Pops

81. If you want a steak and maybe a Bloomin' Onion, head on over to Outback Steakhouse, founded in this country.

☐ **a.** England
☐ **b.** United States
☐ **c.** Australia
☐ **d.** New Zealand

> **Did You Know?** According to legend, the charcoal briquette was invented by Henry Ford and Thomas Edison.

82. If you're eating a hot pepper and you start to freak out from the temperature, this liquid will cool your mouth off almost immediately.

☐ **a.** Water
☐ **b.** Beer
☐ **c.** Milk
☐ **d.** Orange juice

83. There's one thing that makes wine tastings in Utah different from wine tastings anywhere else. What is it?

☐ **a.** The fact that they just plain don't exist.
☐ **b.** By Utah law, all wines must be less than 9 percent alcohol.
☐ **c.** It's illegal to actually swallow the wine.
☐ **d.** Sparkling wine only.

84. This college was founded by a brewer.

☐ **a.** BYU
☐ **b.** Vassar
☐ **c.** Northwestern
☐ **d.** Ithaca

85. This state never ratified the 18th Amendment enacting Prohibition.

☐ **a.** Rhode Island
☐ **b.** Delaware
☐ **c.** Georgia
☐ **d.** Virginia

True Story
In the United States, Prohibition was a major boost to the cruise industry. People hopped on "cruises to nowhere," and could legally drink alcohol as soon as the boat entered international waters.

86. Known as "The Numbers," this NYC restaurant has been featured in more New York–based film productions than any other eatery in the city.

☐ **a.** Forty-Four
☐ **b.** 21
☐ **c.** 3rd Street Diner
☐ **d.** The Lottery Deli

87. Starbucks was started in Seattle in what year?

☐ **a.** 1968
☐ **b.** 1971
☐ **c.** 1984
☐ **d.** 1991

88. The ice cream cake "Fudgy the Whale" is brought to you by whom?

☐ **a.** Ben and Jerry's
☐ **b.** Hood
☐ **c.** Turkey Hill
☐ **d.** Carvel

89. The men on the Discovery Channel reality show *The Deadliest Catch* are out to catch what?

- ☐ **a.** Sharks
- ☐ **b.** Whales
- ☐ **c.** Crab
- ☐ **d.** Tuna

90. When Belushi's Bluto proclaimed, "I'm a zit" in *Animal House*, what food did he use to represent pus?

- ☐ **a.** Clam chowder
- ☐ **b.** Mashed potatoes
- ☐ **c.** Milk
- ☐ **d.** Pasta alfredo

91. Next to KFC, this is the largest chicken restaurant chain in the United States.

- ☐ **a.** Popeyes
- ☐ **b.** Roscoe's
- ☐ **c.** Chick-fil-A
- ☐ **d.** Kenny Rogers

92. What is Worcestershire sauce made of?

- ☐ **a.** Spices and ketchup
- ☐ **b.** Anchovies
- ☐ **c.** Wine
- ☐ **d.** Battery acid

> **Did You Know?** In 1932, Franklin D. Roosevelt ran for president on a pledge to end Prohibition.

93. Fact or Fiction: Drinking Mountain Dew shrinks your balls.

- ☐ **a.** Fact
- ☐ **b.** Fiction

94. Who's responsible for this quote? "Always do sober what you said you'd do drunk. That will teach you to keep your mouth shut."

☐ **a.** Winston Churchill
☐ **b.** W.C. Fields
☐ **c.** Ernest Hemingway
☐ **d.** Dylan Thomas

95. The "special sauce" on a Big Mac has been shown to be basically what?

☐ **a.** Ketchup and vinegar
☐ **b.** Thousand Island dressing
☐ **c.** Russian dressing
☐ **d.** Ranch dressing with onions

96. Frederick the Great of Prussia tried to encourage the use of alcohol while at the same time banning this substance.

☐ **a.** Coffee
☐ **b.** Cranberry juice
☐ **c.** Opium
☐ **d.** Tea

97. This dude was the Greek god of wine.

☐ **a.** Zeus
☐ **b.** Dionysus
☐ **c.** Ares
☐ **d.** Midas

98. Which of the following has not been a McDonald's slogan?

☐ **a.** Food, Folks, and Fun
☐ **b.** You Deserve a Break Today
☐ **c.** Open Up and Say *Yum*
☐ **d.** We Do It All for You

99. You're cooking up spaghetti for a hot date. The lady requests it be cooked al dente. What does that mean?

☐ **a.** Cooked so it's firm
☐ **b.** Cooked without salt
☐ **c.** Cooked longer, so it's soft
☐ **d.** Cooked, then warmed in a skillet

True Story
The first U.S. Marines recruiting station was located in a bar.

100. A bucket of KFC is the perfect thing to nosh on while watching football on a Sunday. How many herbs and spices are in KFC's world famous original recipe?

☐ **a.** Seven
☐ **b.** Nine
☐ **c.** Eleven
☐ **d.** Fifteen

ANSWER KEY
CHAPTER 3. RATIONS: HOT DOGS, BEER, AND MORE

1. b.

2. c.

3. c.

4. b.

5. a.

6. c.

7. a.

8. b.

9. b.

10. c.

11. a.

12. b. J. Wilson of Iowa consumed only beer and water for the period of Lent, showing that it is possible.

13. c.

14. a.

15. a.

16. b. Although this is a popular theory, the truth is nobody seems to know the origin of the "33."

17. i. c; ii. d; iii. e; iv. a; v. b

18. a. A good tequila is made of 100 percent of the stuff.

19. c.

20. a.

21. c.

22. d.

23. c.

24. a. What did you think, we were trying to trick you? We wouldn't do that.

25. c.

26. a.

27. b.

28. b.

29. c.

30. d.

31. c.

32. c.

33. a. Ruth was working at the Toll House Inn when the baking chocolate ran out, and the rest is history.

34. d.

35. b.

36. c.

37. c.

38. b. A copyright issue forced Burger King to adopt a different name when they move to Aussie land.

39. b. Use soft sponges; steel wool will ruin the Teflon coating.

40. a. By act of Congress in 1964.

41. d. It opens the capillaries to fill them with warm blood, making people feel warmer, but in fact it lowers body temperature.

42. b. Other than that, it's the same drink.

43. b.

44. c.

45. c. There's a law in Germany called Reinheitsgebot which requires all beer be made of only water, malt, hops, and yeast. Sam's passed.

46. a.

47. c.

48. d. Wendy's was ahead of the curve, adding their value menu in 1989.

49. c.

50. a.

51. c.

52. a.

53. b.

54. d.

55. d.

56. c.

57. c. Whatever the number, it's worth the effort.

58. a.

59. c.

60. a. Because they looked like men from Mars.

61. b. They certainly know their sweets.

62. c.

63. b.

64. b. *Harold and Kumar Go to White Castle*, with a little help from the god NPH—Neil Patrick Harris.

65. b.

66. d. The record is fifty-seven in fifteen minutes by Takeru Kobayashi—also the world's most famous competitive hot dog eater.

67. c. That's a lot of Big Macs.

68. a.

69. b.

70. b.

71. a.

72. c. Arby's is RB spelled out, short for Raffel Brothers.

73. c. Out of respect for the Hindu faith.

74. a. As a matter of fact, honey found in ancient Egyptian tombs has been eaten and is considered edible!

75. b.

76. a. Brilliant!

77. c. The brother that could never quite live up to expectations.

78. d. And it's big: Pizza Hut is the world's largest user of cheese.

79. d. Who could forget Tony the Tiger?

80. a.

81. b. While the theme is Australian, the company is American.

82. c. The protein found in milk counteracts the peppers' "hotness."

83. c.

84. b.

85. a.

86. b. Its credits include *Wall Street* and *The Associate*.

87. b. And now has well over 16,000 locations for those in need of a quick caffeine fix.

88. d.

89. c.

90. b.

91. c. With over 1,300 locations.

92. b. The small fish are set in vinegar to dissolve into the sauce.

93. b. The inventor, while walking past a radar tube, noticed that the chocolate bar in his pocket melted. He immediately tried popcorn, which as you can imagine, popped.

94. c.

95. b.

96. a.

97. b.

98. c.

99. a.

100. c.

SCORE!

81–100: You're a filet, grilled to perfection. Perfect in every way.

61–80: Pepperoni pizza from Domino's. Good, but not the best around.

41–60: Microwave dinner. Surprisingly good. Certainly not great.

21–40: Ehh. Enjoying that Cosmo you got there?

0–20: You're like two-month-old milk. Just rotten.

CHAPTER 4

STATS: KNOW YOUR NUMBERS

There's nothing guys enjoy more than arguing with other guys; standing at the bar, claiming knowledge of stats, declaring obscure facts to be true. And a lot of that stuff is about numbers—longest home run, fastest car, biggest machine gun. You get the idea. So now it's time we found out . . . do you know your numbers?

1. An average-sized woman (138 pounds) can consume roughly four drinks in four hours to reach a blood alcohol content (BAC) of 0.08. How many drinks can an average-sized man (170 pounds) consume in three hours to reach the same BAC?

☐ **a.** Four
☐ **b.** Five
☐ **c.** Six
☐ **d.** Seven

2. Mt. Everest is how tall?

☐ **a.** 19,190'
☐ **b.** 22,557'
☐ **c.** 29,029'
☐ **d.** 31,330'

> **Did You Know?** In Arizona, it's illegal to keep more than two dildos under one roof.

3. All right, Mr. Pool Shark: what is the length of the average pool cue?

☐ **a.** 37"
☐ **b.** 58"
☐ **c.** 76"
☐ **d.** 90"

4. There are roughly how many shark attack fatalities per year worldwide?

☐ **a.** Ten
☐ **b.** Twenty-five
☐ **c.** Sixty-five
☐ **d.** Eighty

5. Ever been to the NFL Hall of Fame? If not, take a trip—it's worth it. Before you leave, though, make sure you know where you're going. What's the address of the NFL Hall of Fame?

☐ **a.** 2121 George Halas Drive NW Canton, OH
☐ **b.** 25 Main Street Cooperstown, NY
☐ **c.** 1000 Hall of Fame Ave Springfield, MA
☐ **d.** 30 Yonge Street Toronto, Ontario

6. Throwing a party and want to order a keg instead of buying cans? How many twelve-ounce beers are in a keg? You know, so you can plan accordingly.

☐ **a.** 72
☐ **b.** 98
☐ **c.** 160
☐ **d.** 200

7. Americans likes their guns, we all know that. But just how many guns are there in the United States per 100 people?

☐ **a.** Thirty-five
☐ **b.** Fifty
☐ **c.** Seventy-five
☐ **d.** Ninety

8. Time to see if you know your Roman numerals. When we get to Super Bowl Seventy-Seven, what will the logo look like?

☐ **a.** LXXVII
☐ **b.** LIIIXX
☐ **c.** XXVIIL
☐ **d.** LXXIX

9. Mt. Etna, an active volcano, has been continuously erupting for the last how many years?

☐ **a.** 44
☐ **b.** 75
☐ **c.** 850
☐ **d.** 3,500

10. The Challenger Deep in the Mariana Trench of the Pacific Ocean is the deepest point in the world. Just how deep is this abyss?

☐ **a.** 11,374'
☐ **b.** 17,881'
☐ **c.** 35,840'
☐ **d.** 39,459'

11. The Nile River is the longest river in the world. How long is it?

☐ **a.** 2,763 miles
☐ **b.** 3,030 miles
☐ **c.** 4,132 miles
☐ **d.** 6,429 miles

12. How many feet between bases in Major League Baseball?

☐ **a.** 75
☐ **b.** 90
☐ **c.** 110
☐ **d.** 120

13. How many rounds did 1974's "Rumble in the Jungle" last?

☐ **a.** Eight
☐ **b.** Nine
☐ **c.** Ten
☐ **d.** Eleven

14. The Panama Canal was one of the largest projects ever taken on by the U.S. Army Corp of Engineers. Just how long is the thing?

☐ **a.** 15 miles
☐ **b.** 50 miles
☐ **c.** 100 miles
☐ **d.** 125 miles

15. The number of dimples on a golf ball changes from brand to brand, but the diameter does not. So, Tiger, can you tell us what the diameter of an officially sanctioned American golf ball is?

☐ **a.** 1.25 inches
☐ **b.** 1.42 inches
☐ **c.** 1.68 inches
☐ **d.** 2.2 inches

> **Did You Know?** A guy named Les Stewart typed out all the numbers from one to one million. It took him sixteen years.

16. What is the equivalent metric size to a $\frac{7}{16}$-inch wrench?

☐ **a.** 7 mm
☐ **b.** 11 mm
☐ **c.** 13 mm
☐ **d.** 16 mm

17. Ever been dragged to a party by the wife and gotten stuck making small talk? It invariably comes back to the weather. Next time, throw this fact in there—that is, if you know the answer. What is the average temperature of the universe?

☐ **a.** 3° kelvin (roughly –454.6°F)
☐ **b.** 100° kelvin (roughly –269°F)
☐ **c.** 200° kelvin (roughly –99°F)
☐ **d.** –675°F

18. Prepare to have your mind blown: Not everyone takes all their vacation days! Why not? We have no idea. But over in France, they seem to have the right idea. Workers in France take nearly 90 percent of their allotted vacation days. But here in the United States, workers are hovering around this number.

☐ **a.** 24 percent
☐ **b.** 59 percent
☐ **c.** 72 percent
☐ **d.** 81 percent

19. From 1974 until 1998, the Sears Tower was the tallest building in the world at 1,451'. But then a whole crop of new super skyscrapers popped up. Built in 2010, the Burj Khalifa in Dubai is now the tallest in the world, measuring how tall?

☐ **a.** 1,512'
☐ **b.** 1,681'
☐ **c.** 2,716'
☐ **d.** 3,420'

20. What's Jenny's phone number?

☐ **a.** 439–5608
☐ **b.** 867–5309
☐ **c.** 555–9045
☐ **d.** 267–2305

21. All right, Hef, what's the address of the Playboy Mansion (a.k.a. Heaven on Earth).

☐ **a.** 293 Palace Drive, Malibu CA
☐ **b.** 10236 Charing Cross Rd, Los Angeles CA
☐ **c.** 20074 Sunset Blvd, Los Angeles CA
☐ **d.** 69 Hefner Way, Beverly Hills CA

22. In Wilt Chamberlain's second autobiography, he claims to have had sex with how many women in his lifetime?

☐ **a.** 2,500
☐ **b.** 10,000
☐ **c.** 20,000
☐ **d.** 45,000

23. The Steel Dragon 2000 in Japan is the longest roller coaster in the world, traveling how many feet?

☐ **a.** 2,000
☐ **b.** 4,280
☐ **c.** 6,900
☐ **d.** 8,133

> **Did You Know?** Shaquille O'Neal wears size 22 shoes. During his playing days, he wore a brand new pair for every game.

24. The world's fastest roller coaster is the Formula Rossa in Dubai; it travels at this maximum speed.

☐ **a.** 82 mph
☐ **b.** 103 mph
☐ **c.** 149 mph
☐ **d.** 186 mph

25. Since 1986, something called the Self-Transcendence Marathon has been the longest sanctioned foot race in the world. How many miles does it cover?

☐ **a.** 600
☐ **b.** 1,200
☐ **c.** 3,100
☐ **d.** 5,000

26. Opened in 2011, the Jiaozhou Bay Bridge is the longest cross-sea bridge in the world traversed by cars. It stretches across this ridiculous number of miles.

☐ **a.** Eight
☐ **b.** Seventeen
☐ **c.** Twenty-six
☐ **d.** Fifty-one

27. Angel Falls in Venezuela is the tallest waterfall on Earth. It drops how many feet?

☐ **a.** 3,211
☐ **b.** 2,092
☐ **c.** 5,367
☐ **d.** 4,004

28. The highest temperature on Earth was recorded in Libya, circa 1922. How hot was it?

☐ **a.** 112°F
☐ **b.** 125°F
☐ **c.** 136°F
☐ **d.** 151°F

29. The lowest temperature ever recorded on Earth was in Antarctica on July 21, 1983. How cold was it?

   ☐ **a.** −45°F
   ☐ **b.** −100°F
   ☐ **c.** −126°F
   ☐ **d.** −210°F

30. Layering up is important in the winter, but one guy took it to the extreme and set a world record by wearing this many T-shirts at once.

   ☐ **a.** 64
   ☐ **b.** 121
   ☐ **c.** 209
   ☐ **d.** 314

31. The peregrine falcon is the fastest hunting bird in the world. When it dives it can reach speeds of over how many MPH?

   ☐ **a.** 75
   ☐ **b.** 100
   ☐ **c.** 150
   ☐ **d.** 200

32. Like all dogs, the Irish wolfhound is man's best friend. A *big* friend. When standing on its hind legs, this bad boy averages a height of how many feet tall?

   ☐ **a.** Five
   ☐ **b.** Six
   ☐ **c.** Seven
   ☐ **d.** Eight

> **Did You Know?** Need a date? Head to the Big Apple. In the NYC area, there are 200,000 more single women than men.

33. Sir Edmund Hillary was the first man to reach the summit of Mt. Everest. He accomplished the feat in what year?

- ☐ **a.** 1919
- ☐ **b.** 1944
- ☐ **c.** 1953
- ☐ **d.** 1960

34. Fact or Fiction: There are fewer than fifty blimps in the entire world.

- ☐ **a.** Fact
- ☐ **b.** Fiction

35. The blue whale is the largest animal in the sea. How long can these puppies get?

- ☐ **a.** 63'
- ☐ **b.** 79'
- ☐ **c.** 92'
- ☐ **d.** 105'

36. Feeling a little lonely? Don't worry. You're not the only one. In the United States, this many people over the age of eighteen are unmarried.

- ☐ **a.** 52 million
- ☐ **b.** 104 million
- ☐ **c.** 136 million
- ☐ **d.** 208 million

37. How long is the Great Wall of China?

- ☐ **a.** Over 400 miles
- ☐ **b.** Over 1,000 miles
- ☐ **c.** Over 3,000 miles
- ☐ **d.** Over 5,000 miles

38. In what year did Jackie Robinson break the color barrier in baseball?

☐ **a.** 1930
☐ **b.** 1939
☐ **c.** 1947
☐ **d.** 1950

Classic Quote

"Mathematics are well and good but nature keeps dragging us around by the nose."

—ALBERT EINSTEIN

39. Fact or Fiction: Arithmophobia is the fear of numbers.

☐ **a.** Fact
☐ **b.** Fiction

40. How many times is the word "fuck" (and its derivatives, like "motherfucker") used in the 1983 gangster classic *Scarface*?

☐ **a.** 98
☐ **b.** 147
☐ **c.** 226
☐ **d.** 308

True Story
Having over a dollar in change does not guarantee that you can make change for a dollar.

41. What was Marilyn Monroe's bra size?

☐ **a.** 32DD
☐ **b.** 34C
☐ **c.** 36D
☐ **d.** 38E

42. Fact or Fiction: Every year, 100 percent of the atoms in your body are replaced.

☐ **a.** Fact
☐ **b.** Fiction

43. How many names are on the Vietnam War Memorial?

☐ **a.** 26,381
☐ **b.** 49,048
☐ **c.** 58,267
☐ **d.** 61,159

44. So, Mr. Professional, how many business days are there in a year?

☐ **a.** 244
☐ **b.** 260
☐ **c.** 271
☐ **d.** 313

45. On average, how many city blocks do you have to walk to equal a mile?

☐ **a.** Five
☐ **b.** Eight
☐ **c.** Ten
☐ **d.** Fifteen

46. Pittsburgh is sometimes known as the "City of Bridges." How many are we talking about here?

☐ **a.** 62
☐ **b.** 281
☐ **c.** 312
☐ **d.** 446

47. How many ounces are in a "tall boy" beer can?

☐ **a.** Sixteen
☐ **b.** Twenty
☐ **c.** Twenty-four
☐ **d.** Thirty-two

48. What number did Jordan wear after his return to the NBA from a stint playing baseball?

☐ **a.** 23
☐ **b.** 34
☐ **c.** 41
☐ **d.** 45

True Story
The average price for a single acre of land on the Strip in Las Vegas is $27 million.

49. This is the largest ocean in the world at 155,557,000 sq. kilometers.

☐ **a.** Atlantic
☐ **b.** Pacific
☐ **c.** Indian
☐ **d.** Arctic

50. How many number-one hits did the Beatles have in the United States?

☐ **a.** Twelve
☐ **b.** Eighteen
☐ **c.** Twenty-one
☐ **d.** Twenty-seven

51. How many number one hits did Elvis have in the United States?

☐ **a.** Twelve
☐ **b.** Eighteen
☐ **c.** Twenty-one
☐ **d.** Twenty-seven

52. What NASCAR driver drove car #24?

☐ **a.** Jeff Gordon
☐ **b.** Mark Martin
☐ **c.** Richard Petty
☐ **d.** Dale Earnhardt Sr.

53. This guy, sometimes known as "Stink," is arguably the best pro to ever sport #69. Ooh, 69!

☐ **a.** Mark Schlereth
☐ **b.** Bud Graham
☐ **c.** "Smelly" Ed Ernst
☐ **d.** Bart Starr

54. The longest baseball game ever was a showdown between the White Sox and Brewers in 1984. Spanning two days, it ran how many hours long?

☐ **a.** Five
☐ **b.** Six
☐ **c.** Seven
☐ **d.** Eight

55. What is the greatest number of innings ever played in an MLB game?

☐ **a.** Twenty-four innings
☐ **b.** Twenty-five innings
☐ **c.** Twenty-six innings
☐ **d.** Twenty-seven innings

56. What is the largest desert in the world at roughly 14 million sq. kilometers?

☐ **a.** Sahara
☐ **b.** Mojave
☐ **c.** Arabian
☐ **d.** Antarctic

True Story
There are 86,400 seconds in day.

57. The largest earthquake in recorded history hit Chile in 1960 and registered what number on the Richter scale?

☐ **a.** 8.1
☐ **b.** 8.9
☐ **c.** 9.5
☐ **d.** 10.1

58. What is the record for the longest free-fall without being killed?

☐ **a.** 700'
☐ **b.** 4,500'
☐ **c.** 14,000'
☐ **d.** 33,000'

59. The world's largest fish is the whale shark (it's a shark, not a whale). It often grows to be how long?

☐ **a.** 20'
☐ **b.** 35'
☐ **c.** 45'
☐ **d.** 60'

60. The longest title reign by a heavyweight fighter was Joe Louis. Badass Joe defended his title twenty-five times over how many years?

☐ **a.** Five
☐ **b.** Eight
☐ **c.** Eleven
☐ **d.** Fourteen

61. The longest heat wave (consecutive days over 100°F) took place in Australia. It lasted how many days?

☐ **a.** 14
☐ **b.** 56
☐ **c.** 101
☐ **d.** 160

62. As of 2011, British soldier Craig Harrison holds the record for longest confirmed sniper kill, at this many yards.

☐ **a.** 1,413
☐ **b.** 1,887
☐ **c.** 2,109
☐ **d.** 2,707

63. The record for the longest field goal in NFL history is shared by two men, Jason Elam and Tom Dempsey. How many yards?

☐ **a.** Fifty-nine
☐ **b.** Sixty-one
☐ **c.** Sixty-three
☐ **d.** Seventy

64. Robert Pershing Wadlow was the tallest person in modern, recorded history. How tall was he?

☐ **a.** 7'9"
☐ **b.** 8'4"
☐ **c.** 8'11"
☐ **d.** 9'1"

Did You Know? The 27 Club includes famous musicians who died at age twenty-seven:

Robert Johnson
Brian Johnson
Jim Morrison
Janis Joplin
Kurt Cobain
Jimi Hendrix
Amy Winehouse

---

65. The world's longest railroad is the Trans-Siberian, which covers an astonishing number of miles. How many?

☐ **a.** 4,800
☐ **b.** 6,000
☐ **c.** 8,300
☐ **d.** 10,000

66. Everyone knows the Great Barrier Reef is the largest reef in the world, but just how far does it stretch?

☐ **a.** 870 miles
☐ **b.** 1,430 miles
☐ **c.** 2,460 miles
☐ **d.** 5,100 miles

67. The Hundred Years' War was not a continuous engagement, but instead a series of battles with lots of down time. How long did it actually last?

☐ **a.** 98 years
☐ **b.** 100 years
☐ **c.** 116 years
☐ **d.** 122 years

68. If you don't like driving in tunnels, avoid the Laerdal tunnel in Norway, the longest drivable tunnel in the world. It runs how many miles?

☐ **a.** 5.4
☐ **b.** 9.5
☐ **c.** 12.7
☐ **d.** 15.2

69. The tallest tree ever recorded is a redwood tree in California. How tall is it?

☐ **a.** 183'
☐ **b.** 264'
☐ **c.** 379'
☐ **d.** 412'

70. In 2001, a train in Australia set the record for longest train ever. It consisted of this many cars.

☐ **a.** 413
☐ **b.** 531
☐ **c.** 682
☐ **d.** 790

71. Some buildings skip numbering this "unlucky" floor altogether.

   ☐ **a.** Nine
   ☐ **b.** Thirteen
   ☐ **c.** Seventeen
   ☐ **d.** Twenty-one

72. Installing a pool in the yard can be a massive pain in the ass, so just imagine how difficult it was to put in the largest pool ever made. It's located in Chile and is filled entirely with salt water. It measures how long?

   ☐ **a.** 879'
   ☐ **b.** 1,320'
   ☐ **c.** 3,323'
   ☐ **d.** 5,013'

> **Did You Know?** "Four" is the only number in the English language where the number of letters in the name equals the number.

73. What is the longest golf putt recorded in PGA history?

   ☐ **a.** 78"
   ☐ **b.** 92"
   ☐ **c.** 110"
   ☐ **d.** 119"

74. The longest golf putt ever recorded during any event (including non-PGA) was made by Fergus Muir at St. Andrews. During a very gusty day, he sank one from how far?

   ☐ **a.** 175'
   ☐ **b.** 210'
   ☐ **c.** 286'
   ☐ **d.** 375'

75. In 1981, Dudley Wayne Kyzer was given the longest jail sentence in U.S. history for the murder of his wife, his mother-in-law, and a college student in Alabama. How long was that sentence?

☐ **a.** 399 years
☐ **b.** 1,000 years
☐ **c.** 5,200 years
☐ **d.** 10,000 years

76. Not even *War and Peace* comes close to the record held by *Remembrance of Things Past*. The longest novel ever written, this puppy has seven volumes and is roughly how many words long?

☐ **a.** 230,000
☐ **b.** 600,000
☐ **c.** 1 million
☐ **d.** 1.5 million

77. In 2005, a group of clever criminals in Brazil tunneled their way into a bank and made off with the largest sum ever in a bank robbery. What was the size of the take, in U.S. dollars?

☐ **a.** 13.5 million
☐ **b.** 26.2 million
☐ **c.** 71.6 million
☐ **d.** 102.4 million

78. What are the odds of being audited by the IRS, roughly?

☐ **a.** 1 in 100,000
☐ **b.** 1 in 10,000
☐ **c.** 1 in 1000
☐ **d.** 1 in 100

79. We've all seen the scene from *Caddyshack* where the poor old bastard gets struck by lightning in the middle of the greatest round of golf of his life. In reality, what are the odds that you get struck by lightning in a given year?

☐ **a.** 1 in 50,000
☐ **b.** 1 in 250,000
☐ **c.** 1 in 500,000
☐ **d.** 1 in 1 million

80. Roy C. Sullivan is the record holder for most times struck by lightning. How many times has he been struck?

☐ **a.** Three
☐ **b.** Five
☐ **c.** Seven
☐ **d.** Eleven

> **Did You Know?** The original Hawaiian alphabet has only twelve letters.

81. Want two kids without having to deal with a pregnant wife twice? Just have twins. What are the odds of having twins anyway?

☐ **a.** 3 in 100
☐ **b.** 3 in 250
☐ **c.** 3 in 700
☐ **d.** 3 in 1000

82. The odds of hitting the jackpot you're chasing on that slot machine is roughly:

☐ **a.** 1 in 23,223
☐ **b.** 1 in 262,144
☐ **c.** 1 in 789,529
☐ **d.** 1 in 2,467,338

83. The next time you're playing five-card stud and hoping for a royal flush, remember not to hold your breath. The odds of being dealt a royal flush are roughly:

- ☐ **a.** 1 in 389
- ☐ **b.** 1 in 73,256
- ☐ **c.** 1 in 236,433
- ☐ **d.** 1 in 649,739

84. Americans like to chase the American dream (that's why it's called the American dream). Everyone's idea of happiness varies, but it's safe to say that for most of us, becoming a billionaire would qualify. What are the odds of an American being a billionaire?

- ☐ **a.** 1 in 1 million
- ☐ **b.** 1 in 25 million
- ☐ **c.** 1 in 100 million
- ☐ **d.** 1 in 300 million

85. Forget work, that stuff is for fools. Just win the lottery, right? What are the odds of picking a winning Powerball ticket?

- ☐ **a.** 1 in 1,000,000
- ☐ **b.** 1 in 10,375,453
- ☐ **c.** 1 in 147,107,962
- ☐ **d.** 1 in 309,672,954

86. Tokyo is the world's largest city, population wise; can you name the number of residents?

- ☐ **a.** 27 million
- ☐ **b.** 31 million
- ☐ **c.** 36 million
- ☐ **d.** 41 million

87. Remembering the names of your classmates at a high school reunion is tough enough as it is. Imagine going to high school in Rizal High School in Manila, which enrolls this many students annually.

☐ **a.** 5,000
☐ **b.** 15,000
☐ **c.** 25,000
☐ **d.** 40,000

88. Giant clams are the world's largest shellfish, growing to be around how many pounds?

☐ **a.** 75
☐ **b.** 190
☐ **c.** 300
☐ **d.** 500

True Story
Heinz ketchup leaves the bottle at 25 miles per hour.

89. The Library of Congress in Washington, D.C., is the largest library in the world. It houses how many books?

☐ **a.** 10 million
☐ **b.** 30 million
☐ **c.** 45 million
☐ **d.** 60 million

90. What number did Joe DiMaggio wear during his rookie season as a Yankee?

☐ **a.** 3
☐ **b.** 5
☐ **c.** 9
☐ **d.** 11

91. What is the highest recorded score in the arcade game Asteroids?

☐ **a.** 2,435,091
☐ **b.** 12,736,455
☐ **c.** 28,512,690
☐ **d.** 41,336,440

92. Man, it would feel nice to hold a $1,000 bill. But alas, they stopped printing the currency. When?

☐ **a.** 1932
☐ **b.** 1945
☐ **c.** 1951
☐ **d.** 1963

93. This pitcher wore jersey number 17 as an Atlanta Brave, but instead of his last name, he put the word "Channel" on the back of his jersey to promote Channel 17, Ted Turner's TV station.

☐ **a.** Andy Messersmith
☐ **b.** Steve Avery
☐ **c.** Greg Maddux
☐ **d.** Mark Wohlers

94. The king cobra is the longest venomous snake in the world. It regularly reaches this length.

☐ **a.** 8'
☐ **b.** 10'
☐ **c.** 12'
☐ **d.** 15'

95. The next time you complain about the rain, think about Kaneohe Ranch, Oahu, Hawaii. They once reported this many days of consecutive rainfall.

☐ **a.** 93
☐ **b.** 169
☐ **c.** 247
☐ **d.** 432

96. The longest Pink Floyd song is "Atom Heart Mother" which lays it all out for ya in this many minutes.

☐ **a.** Eleven
☐ **b.** Nineteen
☐ **c.** Twenty-three
☐ **d.** Forty-four

Did You Know? According to some sources, 80 percent of all pictures on the Internet are of naked women.

97. Hans Langseth had the distinction of owning the longest beard ever. He had serious stubble, measuring how long?

☐ **a.** 4'
☐ **b.** 9'
☐ **c.** 12'
☐ **d.** 17'

98. The world's smallest antelope has an awesome name: the dik-dik. It's roughly how big?

☐ **a.** twelve pounds
☐ **b.** twenty-five pounds
☐ **c.** forty pounds
☐ **d.** sixty pounds

99. Sport fishing can get pretty intense when you're trying to reel in that big catch. Imagine having to deal with the largest marlin ever caught. This bad boy weighed in at how many pounds?

☐ **a.** 700
☐ **b.** 1,000
☐ **c.** 1,500
☐ **d.** 1,800

100. How many calories are in a McDonald's sausage McMuffin with egg?

☐ **a.** 300
☐ **b.** 350
☐ **c.** 450
☐ **d.** 500

ANSWER KEY
CHAPTER 4. STATS: KNOW YOUR NUMBERS

1. a.

2. c.

3. b.

4. a. Which in our minds, is ten too many. Sharks can suck it.

5. a.

6. c.

7. d.

8. a.

9. d.

10. c. It's pretty dark down there too. Darker than your mother-in-law's foul, rotten soul.

11. c.

12. b.

13. a.

14. b.

15. c.

16. b.

17. a.

18. b.

19. c.

20. b. Tommy Tutone really drilled this one into our heads, huh?

21. b.

22. c.

23. d.

24. c.

25. c. No thanks, have fun though!

26. c.

27. a. Have fun going over that thing in a barrel.

28. c.

29. c.

30. b. He went from 210 pounds to 285 pounds.

31. d.

32. c. Seriously, you could slow dance with one of these things.

33. c.

34. a.

35. d. And can weigh up to 200 tons!

36. b.

37. d. While exact numbers are not known, and some numbers include natural formations, it is generally thought that the wall covers more than 5,000 miles of territory.

38. c.

39. a.

40. c.

41. c.

42. b. More like 98 percent.

43. c. 57,939 were on the wall when it was made in 1982.

44. b. Feels like a helluva lot more, though, don't it?

45. c. It varies by city of course, but ten is a good general measurement.

46. d.

47. a.

48. d.

49. b. As a matter of fact, you could fit the entire Atlantic and Indian Oceans inside the Pacific—or, also, all the land on Earth!

50. d.

51. b. Guess that's why they call him the King . . .

52. a.

53. a.

54. d. The game lasted eight hours and six minutes, totaling twenty-five innings.

55. c. The White Sox and Brewers missed this record by one inning. This twenty-six-inning game was played between the Dodgers and Boston Braves in 1920 and was called a 1–1 tie, due to darkness.

56. d. Technically speaking, Antarctica is a desert because it receives only about 8" of precipitation a year, and beats out the Sahara, which is 9 million sq. kilometers.

57. c. As a point of reference, the Japan quake in 2011 was 8.9, and the Haiti Quake of 2010 was a 7.0.

58. d. Vesna Volovic was aboard the DC9 that was blown up by terrorists over Russia. She fell 33,000 feet onto a snowy slope and eventually was able to walk again. BadASS.

59. c. There are whales that are larger, but whales ain't fish.

60. c. Louis retired after losing to Rocky Marciano in 1951, going 66–3 in his career.

61. d. It stretched from October 31st 1923 to April 7th 1924. The heat's no joke down under.

62. d. That's a big lake, and its deepest point is 4,710'!

63. c. Given that the end zone is ten yards and the ball is placed seven yards behind the line of scrimmage, that means the ball was kicked from the 46 yard line.

64. c. The guy wore a size 37 shoe!

65. b. That's a full ⅓ of Earth's circumference.

66. b.

67. c.

68. d. Needless to say, don't get a flat.

69. c. If not for a pesky woodpecker at the top, they say it would have already broken the 380' mark.

70. c. Hate to be stuck sitting at that railroad crossing.

71. b. Which is so ridiculous . . . call it whatever you want, it's still going to be floor number thirteen!

72. c.

73. c. Jack Nicklaus and Nick Price both sank 110-footers.

74. d. Recognized by Guinness World Records as the longest, Muir used his putter off the tee and sank a hole in one on the par 3.

75. d. We think it's fair to call this one a life sentence.

76. d. Great beach reading for the next seventeen years.

77. c.

78. d. If you make more than $100,000, then the chances increase to roughly 1 in 60.

79. c. If you're still feeling uneasy, the odds of getting struck by lightning and not surviving are 1 in 2.5 million.

80. c. Safe to say most people aren't looking to challenge him for this one.

81. a.

82. b.

83. d.

84. a. Of course, if you live in the rest of the world, the odds jump to 1 in 7 million. So hang tight . . . .

85. c. Still beats work though, right?

86. c.

87. c. Good luck making the varsity squad.

88. d. Anyone got a giant steamer?

89. b. Not to mention millions of newspapers and 50 million manuscripts. And, of course, the crown jewel: a first edition of *Man Enough?*

90. c. He didn't switch to number 5 until his second season.

91. d. By Scott Safran in 1982.

92. b. Grover Cleveland graced the front of the bill.

93. a.

94. d. The largest ever recorded was over 18'. We'll leave that one to Indy.

95. c. The song following it on the album, "Echoes," also runs for twenty-three minutes but loses out by a few seconds.

96. c. August of 1993 to April of 1994.

97. d. Can we get this man a hedge trimmer?

98. a. Hey, we wouldn't complain if we had a twelve-pound dik-dik . . . .

99. d.

100. c. Totally worth it.

SCORE!

81–100: What up, Rain Man?

61–80: Who are you, Chili Palmer? 'Cause you be running these numbers!

41–60: Not bad. You can take heart in this Plato quote: "A good decision is based on knowledge and not on numbers."

21–40: Any chance you're an accountant on Wall Street?

0–20: We fear you may have arithmophobia. Consult your physician.

CHAPTER 5

HISTORY: BECAUSE YOU DON'T WANT TO BE DOOMED TO REPEAT IT

Awesome guy Mark Twain once said, "History is strewn thick with evidence that a truth is not hard to kill, but a lie, well told, Is immortal." The questions that follow will test that idea. See if you can tell the difference between truth and myth. Fancy yourself a regular historian? Then put your money where your mouth is and get crackin'.

1. Ever see the HBO miniseries *Band of Brothers*? It's awe-
    some. Especially on Blu-ray with some surround sound.
    Seriously. You'll be ducking for cover. The true story follows
    soldiers from which WWII division?

    ☐ **a.** 101st Airborne Division, a.k.a. the Screaming Eagles
    ☐ **b.** 2nd Armored Division, a.k.a. Hell on Wheels
    ☐ **c.** 1st Infantry Division, a.ka. the Big Red One
    ☐ **d.** 25th Infantry Division, a.ka. Tropic Lightning

2. On December 7, 1941, the Japanese attacked Pearl Harbor.
    This American president delivered the speech that included
    the now famous line, "Today is a day that will live in infamy."

    ☐ **a.** Teddy Roosevelt
    ☐ **b.** Harry Truman
    ☐ **c.** Franklin D. Roosevelt
    ☐ **d.** Herbert Hoover

    True Story
    In 1918, influenza caused more than 21 million deaths.

3. The invention of gunpowder changed history forever (come
    on, you can't have a great action movie without gunpowder!).
    In which country was gunpowder invented?

    ☐ **a.** China
    ☐ **b.** India
    ☐ **c.** Germany
    ☐ **d.** Russia

4. Okay, we lied. There are actually some pretty badass action
    movies without gunpowder. Which of the following is one of
    them?

    ☐ **a.** *Braveheart*
    ☐ **b.** *The Last Samurai*

☐ **c.** *Ronin*
☐ **d.** *The Patriot*

5. In its relatively short history, the United States has been involved in a helluva lot of wars. Which was the bloodiest, in terms of American lives lost?

   ☐ **a.** Civil War
   ☐ **b.** World War I
   ☐ **c.** World War II
   ☐ **d.** Vietnam

6. This U.S. president was going green long before it was the cool thing to do. He was the first to place solar panels on the White House. They were later removed by Ronald Reagan.

   ☐ **a.** Gerald Ford
   ☐ **b.** Richard Nixon
   ☐ **c.** John F. Kennedy
   ☐ **d.** Jimmy Carter

7. Which Cold War leader was responsible for this quote, on the topic of conflict between the east and west: "There are only two ways: either peaceful coexistence or the most destructive war in history. There is no third way."

   ☐ **a.** Nikita Khrushchev
   ☐ **b.** JFK
   ☐ **c.** Mikhail Gorbachev
   ☐ **d.** Ronald Reagan

Did You Know? In ancient Greece, adulterous men were punished by having a large radish jammed up their rear ends. For real.

---

8. Arr, matey! There've been lots of pirates in the history of the high seas. Which of the following are fictional characters?

- ☐ **a.** Long John Silver
- ☐ **b.** Captain Blood
- ☐ **c.** Dread Pirate Roberts
- ☐ **d.** Blackbeard
- ☐ **e.** Captain Kidd
- ☐ **f.** Black Bart

9. During which war was the White House set on fire?

- ☐ **a.** Revolutionary War
- ☐ **b.** War of 1812
- ☐ **c.** Civil War
- ☐ **d.** French and Indian War

10. The Luftwaffe was what arm of the German forces?

- ☐ **a.** Armored
- ☐ **b.** Infantry
- ☐ **c.** Navy
- ☐ **d.** Air Force

11. Hero-king Leonidas famously led 300 Spartans in a final suicidal stand against a massive Persian army at what battle?

- ☐ **a.** Thermopylae
- ☐ **b.** Sparta
- ☐ **c.** The Hot Gates
- ☐ **d.** Peloponnese

12. This famous author served as a war correspondent (briefly alongside J.D. Salinger) during World War II.

- ☐ **a.** Ernest Hemingway
- ☐ **b.** William Faulkner

☐ **c.** Jack Kerouac
☐ **d.** John Steinbeck

13. D-Day saw Allied forces storming the beaches at Normandy and battling the Nazis on this date in 1944.

☐ **a.** May 20th
☐ **b.** August 3rd
☐ **c.** December 7th
☐ **d.** June 6th

14. Julius Caesar was one of the greatest minds in military history and changed the course of Roman history. He was stabbed to death by his friend (for lack of a better word) who went by this name.

☐ **a.** Mark Antony
☐ **b.** Tiberius Gracchus
☐ **c.** Marcus Brutus
☐ **d.** Cassius Longinus

15. World War II's Battle of the Bulge was fought along this mountain range.

☐ **a.** Alps
☐ **b.** Himalayas
☐ **c.** Ardennes
☐ **d.** Eifel

> **Did You Know?** According to legend, Vikings drank booze out of the skulls of their enemies.

16. Fact or Fiction: Abraham Lincoln, the fifteenth president and slave emancipator, was a Democrat.

☐ **a.** Fact
☐ **b.** Fiction

17. D-Day was a historic invasion of French beaches by Allied troops in 1944. Which beach was not a landing point for the allies?

☐ **a.** Sword
☐ **b.** Juno
☐ **c.** Omaha
☐ **d.** Red

18. What was the name of the gun placement that U.S. Rangers took out to make the D-Day landings possible?

☐ **a.** Cliffs of Gazala
☐ **b.** Arnhem Point
☐ **c.** Pointe du Hoc
☐ **d.** Rattlesnake Ridge

19. The "cricket clicker" used by the 101st Airborne on and after D-Day to tell friend from foe, was originally designed for what use?

☐ **a.** A children's toy
☐ **b.** Keeping time in music
☐ **c.** A bird caller
☐ **d.** A hunting device

20. This U.S. president was a member of the famous cavalry unit the "Rough Riders" before taking office.

☐ **a.** Teddy Roosevelt
☐ **b.** Franklin D. Roosevelt
☐ **c.** Herbert Hoover
☐ **d.** Woodrow Wilson

21. Probably the most famous submachine gun of all time, the Tommy gun was used by gangsters in the '20s and GIs in the '40s. What is the proper name of this weapon?

☐ **a.** M1 Garand
☐ **b.** Thompson M1
☐ **c.** Enfield M1917
☐ **d.** M3A1

22. This U.S. Navy ship survived the attack on Pearl Harbor in World War II. After being sold to the Argentine Navy in 1951, however, it was involved in the Falklands War in 1982 and sunk by the British.

☐ **a.** USS *Phoenix*
☐ **b.** USS *Arizona*
☐ **c.** USS *Massachusetts*
☐ **d.** USS *Langley*

23. FBI agent Joe Pistone (whose life is the basis of the movie *Donnie Brasco*) was responsible for putting away over 120 members of this crime family.

☐ **a.** Bonanno
☐ **b.** Gambino
☐ **c.** Colombo
☐ **d.** Patriarca

24. The Valentine's Day Massacre is the name for the famous killing of seven of Bugs Moran's crew in Chicago at the hands of this gangster's crew.

☐ **a.** Tom Egan
☐ **b.** Frank Nitti
☐ **c.** Al Capone
☐ **d.** Lucky Luciano

25. This gangster helped the U.S. Navy stave off U-boat attacks along the east coast—from his jail cell.

    ☐ **a.** Al Capone
    ☐ **b.** "Machine Gun" Kelly
    ☐ **c.** Salvatore Maranzano
    ☐ **d.** Lucky Luciano

26. Fact or Fiction: Vikings (not the NFL team) are awesome badass warriors.

    ☐ **a.** Fact
    ☐ **b.** Fiction

27. Which state was the first to secede from the union at the start of the Civil War?

    ☐ **a.** Alabama
    ☐ **b.** Georgia
    ☐ **c.** Mississippi
    ☐ **d.** South Carolina

28. Which of these Civil War generals fought for the Confederacy?

    ☐ **a.** Ulysses S. Grant
    ☐ **b.** James Longstreet
    ☐ **c.** William Tecumseh Sherman
    ☐ **d.** Thomas "Stonewall" Jackson
    ☐ **e.** Robert E. Lee
    ☐ **f.** George Armstrong Custer

29. Fact or Fiction: Stonewall Jackson was killed by enemy troops at the Battle of Chancellorsville.

☐ **a.** Fact
☐ **b.** Fiction

30. The Battle of Gettysburg, one of the bloodiest battles of all time, lasted three days and produced how many casualties?

☐ **a.** 11,000
☐ **b.** 23,000
☐ **c.** 40,000
☐ **d.** 50,000

31. Fact or Fiction: Although it didn't shoot an aerodynamic load, the musket was a very accurate weapon due to its high velocity.

☐ **a.** Fact
☐ **b.** Fiction

32. In ancient Rome the term "gladiator" was derived from the word *gladius*, which was Latin for what?

☐ **a.** Soldier
☐ **b.** Sword
☐ **c.** Slave
☐ **d.** Battle

True Story
One of the first-known contraceptives was crocodile dung.

33. Fact or Fiction: Australia was originally a massive penal colony for Britain.

☐ **a.** Fact
☐ **b.** Fiction

34. Fact or Fiction: The reason the British started sending criminals to Australia is because they had just lost what they considered to be a great penal colony, America.

☐ **a.** Fact
☐ **b.** Fiction

35. Fact or Fiction: *Saving Private Ryan* is a true story about Private Wesley Ryan, who lost all his brothers in the war, and the group that searched for him.

☐ **a.** Fact
☐ **b.** Fiction

36. Fact or Fiction: The legendary gladiator Spartacus was a real man.

☐ **a.** Fact
☐ **b.** Fiction

37. Doc Holiday was a famous Wild West gunslinger. You might know him from Val Kilmer's super-cool portrayal in *Tombstone*. What was Doc's first name?

☐ **a.** John
☐ **b.** Henry
☐ **c.** Daniel
☐ **d.** Robert

38. "For What It's Worth" is a classic Vietnam-era song. It's been featured in tons of movies, including *Forrest Gump*. Who sang it?

☐ **a.** The Rolling Stones
☐ **b.** Creedence Clearwater Revival
☐ **c.** Buffalo Springfield
☐ **d.** Jefferson Airplane

39. Fact or Fiction: "For What It's Worth" is a protest song about Vietnam.

    ☐ **a.** Fact
    ☐ **b.** Fiction

40. Can you imagine having to change the channels without a remote? Sounds miserable, right? The first remote control device was invented in 1955. What was it called?

    ☐ **a.** Your Friendly Remote
    ☐ **b.** The Lazy Bones
    ☐ **c.** The Flashmatic
    ☐ **d.** The Electro Dial

Did You Know? According to legend, the first bomb dropped on Germany in WWII killed the only elephant in the Berlin zoo.

---

41. Match the famous Native American leader with his tribe.

    ☐ **i.** Sitting Bull   **a.** Shawnee
    ☐ **ii.** Tecumseh   **b.** Apache
    ☐ **iii.** Geronimo   **c.** Sioux

42. Math class can be a breeze with a calculator. But that's only because they're so easy to carry around! It wasn't always that way. The first all-transistor calculator by IBM cost $83,210 and weighed in at around:

    ☐ **a.** 29 pounds
    ☐ **b.** 130 pounds
    ☐ **c.** 1,270 pounds
    ☐ **d.** 2,400 pounds

43. Whatever DIY project you plan to tackle next will be a lot easier with a power drill, maybe the most important power tool in a guy's workshop. It was invented by Black & Decker in what year?

☐ **a.** 1917
☐ **b.** 1924
☐ **c.** 1936
☐ **d.** 1941

44. We've definitely heard "hey, your zipper is down" more than once in our lives. What year were zippers invented?

☐ **a.** 1822
☐ **b.** 1887
☐ **c.** 1913
☐ **d.** 1939

45. The charcoal grill has been a staple of cookouts since its invention in what year?

☐ **a.** 1908
☐ **b.** 1933
☐ **c.** 1951
☐ **d.** 1960

46. Which man was *not* a crew member of the Apollo 11 mission, the first mission to land on the moon?

☐ **a.** Neil Armstrong
☐ **b.** Edwin "Buzz" Aldrin Jr.
☐ **c.** William A. Anders
☐ **d.** Michael Collins

47. Vasily Zaitsev was a Russian sniper during WWII who, during the invasion of Stalingrad, had forty confirmed kills in the period of ten days. This movie tells his story.

☐ **a.** *Sniper*
☐ **b.** *Enemy at the Gates*
☐ **c.** *Behind Enemy Lines*
☐ **d.** *Shooter*

48. Which of these mob movies follows the life of real-life gangster Henry Hill?

☐ **a.** *Casino*
☐ **b.** *A Bronx Tale*
☐ **c.** *Goodfellas*
☐ **d.** *The Untouchables*

> **True Story**
> When the ancient Egyptians defeated Libya in thirteenth century B.C. they returned home with 13,230 penises as prizes.

49. Ridley Scott's 2001 *Black Hawk Down* tells the true story of which battle?

☐ **a.** Battle of Khafji
☐ **b.** Battle of the Bridges
☐ **c.** Battle of Mogadishu
☐ **d.** Battle of Fallujah

50. Arrange these military ranks in order from lowest to highest:

☐ **i.** Sergeant	**a.** 1
☐ **ii.** Private	**b.** 2
☐ **iii.** General	**c.** 3
☐ **iv.** Captain	**d.** 4
☐ **v.** Corporal	**e.** 5
☐ **vi.** Major	**f.** 6

51. After bombing Pearl Harbor, the Japanese tried placing an air strip on which of these islands, which the United States defended earning their first land victory over Japan?

☐ **a.** Midway
☐ **b.** Guadalcanal
☐ **c.** Wake Island
☐ **d.** Makin Atoll

52. The movie *Catch Me If You Can* is based on the real-life story of what confidence man who, among other things, forged checks during the 1960s?

☐ **a.** Frank Abagnale
☐ **b.** John Treante
☐ **c.** Matthew N. McArdle
☐ **d.** Timothy Quagmire

53. Fact or Fiction: In 1925, con man Victor Lustig sold the Eiffel Tower to an unwitting buyer.

☐ **a.** Fact
☐ **b.** Fiction

54. Fact or Fiction: Michelangelo sold a fake antique cupid he had carved, aged and all, to a cardinal in 1496.

☐ **a.** Fact
☐ **b.** Fiction

55. This newspaper published a Pulitzer Prize–winning article in 1982 that turned out, much to their dismay, to be made up.

☐ **a.** *New York Times*
☐ **b.** *Los Angeles Times*
☐ **c.** *Miami Herald*
☐ **d.** *Washington Post*

56. At Andrew Jackson's funeral, his pet parrot was in attendance but had to be removed for what?

☐ **a.** Singing
☐ **b.** Crapping on the casket
☐ **c.** Swearing
☐ **d.** Flying into guests

True Story
Andrew Jackson dueled a man after he insulted Jackson's wife. The other man, Charles Dickinson, fired first and hit Jackson in the chest, but Jackson stood fast, fired, and killed Dickinson. Jackson never had the bullet removed.

57. The *Enola Gay* is famous for being the plane that dropped an atomic bomb on Hiroshima. What is the name of the plane that dropped the second bomb on Nagasaki?

☐ **a.** Hillbilly Sal
☐ **b.** Bocks Car
☐ **c.** Bulldog Billy
☐ **d.** Steel Hammer

58. Fact or Fiction: During the Civil War there were no Medal of Honor recipients among the 200,000 African Americans serving in the Union army.

☐ **a.** Fact
☐ **b.** Fiction

59. When Columbus landed in the new world, where did he land?

☐ **a.** Plymouth Rock, Massachusetts
☐ **b.** Key West, Florida
☐ **c.** Bermuda Island
☐ **d.** Salvador Island, Bahamas

60. George Washington was elected the first president of the United States in what year?

☐ **a.** 1776
☐ **b.** 1789
☐ **c.** 1791
☐ **d.** 1801

Did You Know? In the Middle Ages, people thought intelligence lived in the heart, not the brain.

61. What action represents the origin of the current-day military salute?

☐ **a.** Knights opening the visors on their helmets when they passed the king
☐ **b.** British Navy crewmen facing their palms down to conceal dirty gloves
☐ **c.** Romans approaching officials with their hand raised to show lack of a weapon
☐ **d.** All of the above

62. Some people speculate that America was discovered long before Columbus by this culture, after finding coins and artifacts that date back to before the birth of Christ.

☐ **a.** Vikings
☐ **b.** Romans
☐ **c.** Chinese
☐ **d.** Mongols

63. The Miss America pageant was originally created to serve what purpose?

☐ **a.** Extend tourism past Labor Day in Atlantic City
☐ **b.** Counteract the effects of woman's lib

☐ **c.** Create one unifying governing body for beauty contests
☐ **d.** Get laid

64. Ten U.S. presidents did not have a college degree, but this man was the only one since 1900.

☐ **a.** John F. Kennedy
☐ **b.** Teddy Roosevelt
☐ **c.** Harry Truman
☐ **d.** Ronald Reagan

True Story
The electric chair was invented by a dentist.

65. Saddam Hussein—you remember him, right? The former dictator of Iraq? He was given the key to this city in 1980.

☐ **a.** Moscow
☐ **b.** Detroit
☐ **c.** Paris
☐ **d.** Havana

66. Bayer, makers of aspirin, marketed this drug in the 1890s.

☐ **a.** Cocaine
☐ **b.** Marijuana
☐ **c.** Opium
☐ **d.** Heroin

67. Which is *not* one of the Seven Wonders of the Ancient World?

☐ **a.** Statue of Zeus at Olympia
☐ **b.** Lighthouse at Alexandria
☐ **c.** Colossus of Rhodes
☐ **d.** The Bust of Maximus in Kathmandu

68. Fact or Fiction: Privateers were pirates commissioned by the crown to steal from enemy ships, so long as they gave half of their plunder to the crown.

☐ **a.** Fact
☐ **b.** Fiction

69. The motto of the Marines, *Semper Fidelis*, is Latin for what?

☐ **a.** Always faithful
☐ **b.** Always ready
☐ **c.** Always prepared
☐ **d.** Always brothers

70. The Merchant Royal is a famous shipwreck for what reason?

☐ **a.** It was lost during battle and never found.
☐ **b.** It was the first reported missing in the Bermuda Triangle.
☐ **c.** It was carrying an assload of money and treasure.
☐ **d.** It was supposed to be an unsinkable ship.

71. Founding father Alexander Hamilton was killed by Aaron Burr in what fashion?

☐ **a.** Hanging
☐ **b.** Fist fight
☐ **c.** Duel
☐ **d.** Drowning

> **Did You Know?** John Wilkes Booth's brother once saved the life of Abraham Lincoln's son.

72. The Zimmerman Telegraph was a transmission sent from Germany to Mexico in 1917, but was intercepted by the United States. What did the telegraph ask of Mexico?

☐ **a.** To attack the United States
☐ **b.** To make it appear as if their army had been weakened by attack
☐ **c.** To send food to Germany
☐ **d.** All of the above

73. For roughly $15 million, the United States purchased the Louisiana Territory from Napoleon. The land in the deal accounts for what fraction of the U.S.?

☐ **a.** ½
☐ **b.** ⅓
☐ **c.** ⅕
☐ **d.** ¹⁄₁₀

74. It is estimated that the first smelting of iron took place when?

☐ **a.** 1400 B.C.
☐ **b.** 600 B.C.
☐ **c.** A.D. 400
☐ **d.** A.D. 1500

75. John Bardeen, Walter H. Brattain, and William Shockley invented this cornerstone of modern electronics in 1948.

☐ **a.** Microchip
☐ **b.** Battery
☐ **c.** Transistor
☐ **d.** Vacuum tubes

76. This war was considered groundbreaking because people could watch it live on TV.

□ **a.** Korean
□ **b.** Vietnam
□ **c.** Falklands
□ **d.** Gulf

77. How did Erwin Rommel, known as the Desert Fox for his work as a German Field Marshall during World War II, die?

□ **a.** Committed suicide to avoid trial for the attempted assassination of Hitler
□ **b.** Shot in the back by German officer Wilhelm Burgdorf
□ **c.** Succumbed to wounds suffered from an allied attack on his staff car
□ **d.** Executed by hanging at the Nuremberg trials

78. Fact or Fiction: According to a Veterans Administration study, drug use among Vietnam veterans is higher than that of nonvets.

□ **a.** Fact
□ **b.** Fiction

79. Most of the men who served in Vietnam were:

□ **a.** Drafted
□ **b.** College students
□ **c.** Volunteers
□ **d.** Over thirty years old

80. During the Kent State protests of the Vietnam War, four people were killed. What state is the college located in?

□ **a.** Iowa
□ **b.** Ohio

☐ **c.** Maryland
☐ **d.** Texas

Did You Know? Until President Kennedy was killed, it wasn't a federal crime to assassinate the president.

81. This American really pissed some people off when she posed with a North Vietnamese anti-aircraft gun.

☐ **a.** Jane Fonda
☐ **b.** Mary Tyler Moore
☐ **c.** Cher
☐ **d.** Diane Keaton

82. Heroin kingpin Frank Lucas (played by Denzel Washington in the movie *American Gangster*) purports to have smuggled heroin into the United States on this man's airplane.

☐ **a.** Richard Nixon
☐ **b.** Lyndon B. Johnson
☐ **c.** Henry Kissinger
☐ **d.** William Westmoreland

83. The Vietnam War ended in 1973. What year were the Pentagon Papers published?

☐ **a.** 1969
☐ **b.** 1971
☐ **c.** 1973
☐ **d.** 1975

84. Fact or Fiction: Maybe the most famous rifle in history, the Winchester was originally called the Henry, after its inventor.

☐ **a.** Fact
☐ **b.** Fiction

85. The skyscraper was invented in what city?

☐ **a.** Boston
☐ **b.** New York
☐ **c.** Chicago
☐ **d.** Philadelphia

86. Albert Sabin developed the polio vaccine in what year?

☐ **a.** 1949
☐ **b.** 1957
☐ **c.** 1960
☐ **d.** 1970

87. Fiber-optic cable was created in 1970 by this company.

☐ **a.** AT&T
☐ **b.** GTE
☐ **c.** Corning Glass
☐ **d.** General Electric

88. Fact or Fiction: The 1983 *Time* magazine "Man of the Year" was not a man at all.

☐ **a.** Fact
☐ **b.** Fiction

> **Did You Know?** Napoleon sketched out his battle plans in a sandbox—just like in the movies!

89. President John Tyler was the first vice president to be elevated to the presidency. His detractors dubbed him with this nickname.

☐ **a.** Oopsi Tyler
☐ **b.** His Accidency
☐ **c.** No Votes John
☐ **d.** Tyrant Tyler

90. This U.S. President had the nickname "The Dude President."

☐ **a.** Theodore Roosevelt
☐ **b.** Chester A. Arthur
☐ **c.** Thomas Jefferson
☐ **d.** Andrew Johnson

91. The first American subway system opened in 1897 in what city?

☐ **a.** Boston
☐ **b.** New York
☐ **c.** Philadelphia
☐ **d.** Washington, D.C.

92. How long after the writing of the Constitution was the Bill of Rights added?

☐ **a.** One year
☐ **b.** Two years
☐ **c.** Five years
☐ **d.** Nine years

93. *Air Force One* is well known to be the presidential plane. But who was the first president to have his plane named that?

☐ **a.** Franklin Roosevelt
☐ **b.** John F. Kennedy
☐ **c.** Richard Nixon
☐ **d.** Jimmy Carter

94. Before there was *Air Force One*, this plane was used.

☐ **a.** Lady Hawk
☐ **b.** Flying Stallion
☐ **c.** Sacred Cow
☐ **d.** Presidential Air

95. Fact or Fiction: The Falklands War was the shortest in recorded history.

☐ **a.** Fact
☐ **b.** Fiction

True Story
Nearly 40 percent of Americans can trace at least one ancestor to Ellis Island.

96. Arab terrorists took Israeli hostages at what event in 1972?

☐ **a.** World Cup
☐ **b.** Republican National Convention
☐ **c.** Olympics
☐ **d.** Running of the Bulls

97. Outlaw Jesse James rolled with a heavy crew, one member of which was his brother, who went by this name.

☐ **a.** Ardle James
☐ **b.** Tom James
☐ **c.** Cletus James
☐ **d.** Frank James

98. During WWII, the Mark II frag grenade was sometimes referred to as what?

☐ **a.** Pineapple
☐ **b.** Jelly bean
☐ **c.** Hot tamale
☐ **d.** Apple cider

99. During WWII, the term "glory boys" referred to whom?

☐ **a.** Marines
☐ **b.** Rangers
☐ **c.** SEALs
☐ **d.** Pilots

100. The Berlin Wall was constructed in this year, in order to prevent people from leaving East Germany.

☐ **a.** 1943
☐ **b.** 1951
☐ **c.** 1958
☐ **d.** 1961

Did You Know? Yellowstone was the world's first national park. It was dedicated in 1872.

ANSWER KEY
CHAPTER 5. HISTORY: BECAUSE YOU DON'T WANT TO BE DOOMED TO REPEAT IT

1. a.

2. c.

3. a.

4. a.

5. a.

6. d.

7. a.

8. a, b, and c

9. b.

10. d.

11. a.

12. a.

13. d.

14. c.

15. c.

16. b.

17. d.

18. c. Army Rangers came in the night before, scaled a vertical cliff, and took care of business.

19. b. Big bands used it in the 1920s.

20. a.

21. b.

22. a.

23. a.

24. c.

25. d. When U.S. intelligence was stumped, they turned to Lucky, who got the word out to his dock worker friends. Not long after, eight German spies were busted.

26. a.

27. d.

28. b, d, and e

29. b. He was killed in the battle, but by his own men, who mistook him for an enemy soldier.

30. d. Read the brilliant *The Killer Angels* for a gripping account of the battle.

31. b. The musket was a wildly inaccurate gun. There's a reason it was replaced.

32. b.

33. a.

34. a. The British had been sending criminals to the United States for years to work off their sentences, but when they lost the Revolutionary War, Australia was suddenly very attractive.

35. b. It was loosely based on the story of Fritz Niland, who lost his brothers during the war. There was no search for him, however, so he was sent home to serve as an MP for the remainder of the war.

36. a. He led a rebellion of slaves against the empire before being killed in battle.

37. a.

38. c.

39. b. It's a protest song, just not about Vietnam. It was written days after a protest in Hollywood over tension between police and young people attending rock clubs in the area.

40. c.

41. i. c; ii. a; iii. b

42. d.

43. a.

44. c.

45. c.

46. c.

47. b.

48. c.

49. c.

50. i. c; ii. a; iii. f; iv. d; v. b; vi. e

51. b. United States perseverance here set the tone for the war in the Pacific theatre.

52. a. He later became a consultant for the government, showing them how to nab forgers.

53. a.

54. a. When the cardinal found out, he was not upset, but amazed at Michelangelo's obvious talent and let him keep the profit.

55. d. Janet Cooke's story about an eight-year-old crack addict turned out to be a work of fiction.

56. c. Who are we to tell the parrot how to grieve?

57. b.

58. b.

59. d. Nope, he did not land in the United States.

60. b.

61. d. All of these actions are considered possible precursors to the current military salute.

62. b.

63. a. Thank you very much, tourism.

64. c. He attended law school, but never earned a degree.

65. b.

66. d. They even trademarked the name.

67. d. Yeah, that's not a real thing. The other four wonders are the Pyramids, the Mausoleum at Halicarnassus, the Hanging Gardens of Babylon and the Temple of Artemis at Ephesus.

68. a. Sir Francis Drake was a privateer later knighted for his services.

69. a.

70. c. An American company is rumored to have found the ship after reporting finding over $500,000 in gold coins on a ship-wreck in the Atlantic. If it was the same boat, that would mean there is still a lot more down there.

71. c. The most famous duel in history.

72. a. It pissed the Americans off a little bit, and helped secure their involvement in WWI.

73. c.

74. a.

75. c. Presumably so that you could read this on your eReader sixty years later.

76. d.

77. a.

78. b.

79. c. Two thirds of all those who served were volunteers, not draftees as some people believe.

80. b. Haven't you ever heard the song "Ohio" by CSNY?

81. a. It didn't help that she also criticized U.S. servicemen on the radio while there.

82. c.

83. b. Daniel Ellsberg leaked the papers in an effort to help bring an end to the war.

84. a. It was invented by B. Tyler Henry of Winchester arms company.

85. c. Many daring architectural projects were undertaken after the Great Fire of 1871, and this one caught on *big* time. Get it, big?

86. b. He saved many lives in the process.

87. c. Thank goodness, what would we do without it?

88. a. The 1983 "man" of the year was the PC, or, personal computer.

89. b.

90. b. For his love of fancy attire.

91. a.

92. b. It didn't take the forefathers long to realize they missed a few things.

93. b.

94. c. This was the first presidential plane, and it was later used by Harry Truman.

95. b. While the war was short at seventy-four days, it cannot compete with the Anglo-Zanzibar war which lasted only thirty-eight minutes!

96. c.

97. d.

98. a.

99. b.

100. d.

SCORE!

81–100: Einstein personified. You, my friend, are truly brilliant!

61–80: Not bad. You're just a few pushups away from being a helluva soldier.

41– 60: We'll call you Switzerland. A nonparticipant.

21–40: This section went about as well for you as Custer's Last Stand went for ol' Custer.

0–20: Someone get this man an invitation to the Darwin Awards.

CHAPTER 6

TELEVISION: THE BOOB TUBE

Most guys enjoy TV. Why not? It beams stuff like *Baywatch*, football, and Al Bundy directly into our homes, twenty-four hours a day, seven days a week. Really, what's not to love? That said, let's see how well you pay attention when you're staring at the boob tube. Time to test your (testicular) television aptitude!

1. You probably know Michael Chiklis as the bald-headed, ultrabadass cop from the FX series *The Shield*. But years earlier, he actually starred on another cop drama. Name that show.

   ☐ **a.** *The Commish*
   ☐ **b.** *NYPD Blue*
   ☐ **c.** *Homicide: Life on the Street*
   ☐ **d.** *Walker, Texas Ranger*

2. This *Godfather* actor also co-starred in the '70s police drama Barney Miller.

   ☐ **a.** James Caan
   ☐ **b.** Abe Vigoda
   ☐ **c.** Richard S. Castellano
   ☐ **d.** Al Lettieri

3. Which duo was better at giving men exactly what they wanted for a half hour every week on Comedy Central's *The Man Show*?

   ☐ **a.** Jimmy Kimmel and Adam Carolla
   ☐ **b.** Joe Rogan and Doug Stanhope

True Story

In its first run, *Baywatch* was cancelled after the first season.

---

4. In the 1980s, every guy wanted to be Thomas Magnum, star of *Magnum P.I.*, as played by Tom Selleck. The only thing slicker than Magnum was his ride. What kind of car was it?

   ☐ **a.** Ferrari Testarossa
   ☐ **b.** Lamborghini Countach
   ☐ **c.** Lamborghini Silhouette
   ☐ **d.** Ferrari 308 GTS

5. In *The Sopranos*, what is Christopher's relation to Tony Soprano?

☐ **a.** Nephew
☐ **b.** Brother
☐ **c.** Cousin
☐ **d.** Son

6. On *Seinfeld*, this *Curb Your Enthusiasm* star played the role of George Steinbrenner—though we never saw his face!

☐ **a.** Jeff Garlin
☐ **b.** Larry David
☐ **c.** Ted Danson
☐ **d.** Richard Lewis

7. Bear Grylls wrestles lizards with his bare hands, swims in freezing water, and sleeps inside of animals Skywalker style—all just to show us regular losers how to survive on this popular show.

☐ **a.** *Out of the Wild*
☐ **b.** *Survivor Man*
☐ **c.** *Dual Survival*
☐ **d.** *Man vs. Wild*

8. *SportsCenter* is a staple man show. Can you tell us which longtime ESPN personality and *SportsCenter* host has a lazy eye due to an injury from an errant football at Jets minicamp?

☐ **a.** Chris Berman
☐ **b.** Scott Van Pelt
☐ **c.** Steve Levy
☐ **d.** Stuart Scott

9. Meg Griffin on *Family Guy* is voiced by what major hottie?

- ☐ **a.** Jill Goodacre
- ☐ **b.** Emmanuelle Chriqui
- ☐ **c.** Mila Kunis
- ☐ **d.** Jessica Biel

10. *Sons of Anarchy* follows a motorcycle club in northern California as they break bones, break the law, and generally break the rules. This *Married with Children* star co-stars.

- ☐ **a.** Christina Applegate
- ☐ **b.** Ed O'Neill
- ☐ **c.** Katey Sagal
- ☐ **d.** David Faustino

11. Action star and pillar of manliness Bruce Willis starred in this private eye sitcom with Cybill Shepherd.

- ☐ **a.** *Moonlighting*
- ☐ **b.** *Mannix*
- ☐ **c.** *Hart to Hart*
- ☐ **d.** *The McLaine Files*

12. This beloved show is the longest-running sitcom in television history.

- ☐ **a.** *The Honeymooners*
- ☐ **b.** *Frasier*
- ☐ **c.** *Seinfeld*
- ☐ **d.** *The Simpsons*

13. Jack Bauer is the super-badass hero from what TV series?

- ☐ **a.** *24*
- ☐ **b.** *Prison Break*
- ☐ **c.** *Miami Vice*
- ☐ **d.** *Lost*

14. *A Few Good Men* ("You can't handle the truth!") and *West Wing* writer Aaron Sorkin also wrote this half-hour, short-lived dramedy featuring Felicity Huffman and Peter Krause in 1998.

    ☐ **a.** *Becker*
    ☐ **b.** *Spin City*
    ☐ **c.** *Sports Night*
    ☐ **d.** *Sex and the City*

15. *Home Improvement* featured Tim Allen as host of the show-within-a-show *Tool Time*. What was the name of his beflanneled assistant on *Tool Time*?

    ☐ **a.** Greg "Household" Gifford
    ☐ **b.** Tom Robbins
    ☐ **c.** Norm Abram
    ☐ **d.** Al Borland

16. This *Diff'rent Strokes* actor, who was tried on murder charges, made headlines of a different kind in 2001 when he was credited with saving a wheelchair-bound woman from drowning.

    ☐ **a.** Gary Coleman
    ☐ **b.** Todd Bridges
    ☐ **c.** Conrad Bain
    ☐ **d.** Dana Plato

17. This *Friends* star was once featured in a music video for Bruce Springsteen, showing off some fancy dance moves.

☐ **a.** Matthew Perry
☐ **b.** Jennifer Aniston
☐ **c.** Matt LeBlanc
☐ **d.** Courtney Cox

18. This actor had a near-continuous spot on TV for thirty years, starring in shows like *Bonanza* and *Little House on the Prairie*. Who is he?

☐ **a.** Michael Landon
☐ **b.** Lorne Greene
☐ **c.** Bill Cartwright
☐ **d.** Burt Reynolds

19. What type of alcohol does the Tim Meadows character, The Ladies' Man, drink on *Saturday Night Live*?

☐ **a.** Alize
☐ **b.** Courvoisier
☐ **c.** Brandy
☐ **d.** Martinis

20. Which of the following comedians was *not* a member of the *Saturday Night Live* cast?

☐ **a.** Eddie Murphy
☐ **b.** Steve Martin
☐ **c.** Bill Murray
☐ **d.** Chris Farley

21. This U.S. Senator was a longtime writer, and sometimes performer, on *Saturday Night Live*.

☐ **a.** John McCain
☐ **b.** Dick Durbin

☐ **c.** Al Franken
☐ **d.** Scott Brown

22. This historic show debuted on September 21st, 1970.

☐ **a.** *Saturday Night Live*
☐ **b.** *60 Minutes*
☐ **c.** *Monday Night Football*
☐ **d.** *Good Morning, America*

23. This man famously announced the death of John Lennon on air during a *Monday Night Football* broadcast.

☐ **a.** Howard Cosell
☐ **b.** Frank Gifford
☐ **c.** Don Meredith
☐ **d.** Walter Cronkite

24. The iconic exterior shot of the bar *Cheers* on the show of the same name actually shows this Boston bar.

☐ **a.** The Black Rose
☐ **b.** Sully's Tap
☐ **c.** Cosmos Bar and Grill
☐ **d.** Bull and Finch Pub

> **Did You Know?** One in every four Americans has appeared on television!

25. What was the name of the con man played by Harry Anderson on *Cheers*?

☐ **a.** Leo
☐ **b.** Tony
☐ **c.** Woody
☐ **d.** Harry

26. This actor won an Emmy for his work on the classic TV show *The Honeymooners*.

☐ **a.** Jackie Gleason
☐ **b.** Art Carney
☐ **c.** Fred Flintstone
☐ **d.** Morey Amsterdam

27. Which of these characters was not part of the over-the-top action-adventures of the A-Team (The *real* A-Team, ya know, from the '80s).

☐ **a.** Hannibal
☐ **b.** Faceman
☐ **c.** B.A.
☐ **d.** Luther

28. Which *A-Team* character was played by Mr. T?

☐ **a.** Murdock
☐ **b.** Hannibal
☐ **c.** Faceman
☐ **d.** B.A.

29. This bouncy *Baywatch* babe was also smoking hot in her starring role alongside Scott Baio on *Charles in Charge*.

☐ **a.** Nicole Eggert
☐ **b.** Pamela Anderson
☐ **c.** Yasmine Bleeth
☐ **d.** Kelly Packard

30. Fact or Fiction: Stan and Kyle's parents from *South Park* are based on creators Matt Stone and Trey Parker's parents.

☐ **a.** Fact
☐ **b.** Fiction

31. Fact or Fiction: Formerly Studio 33, *The Price Is Right* studio is now known as The Bob Barker Studio.

☐ **a.** Fact
☐ **b.** Fiction

32. How many years did Bob Barker host *The Price Is Right*?

☐ **a.** Sixteen
☐ **b.** Twenty-two
☐ **c.** Thirty-five
☐ **d.** Forty

Top 5 List

Our five favorite TV neighbors:

Kramer in *Seinfeld*
Ned Flanders in *The Simpsons*
Wilson Wilson in *Home Improvement*
Larry Dallas in *Three's Company*
Steve Urkel in *Family Matters*

---

33. Ken Jennings is the greatest *Jeopardy!* champion of all time, raking in a whopping $2,520,700 during his amazing seventy-four-game winning streak. That's the most money ever won on a game show. In second place is the $2,180,000, won by Kevin Olmstead on this game show.

☐ **a.** *Deal or No Deal*
☐ **b.** *Wheel of Fortune*
☐ **c.** *Family Feud*
☐ **d.** *Who Wants to Be a Millionaire?*

34. *Cheers* regular Cliff Clavin made his living as a what?

☐ **a.** Bartender
☐ **b.** Mail carrier
☐ **c.** Cop
☐ **d.** Accountant

35. This one-time *Monday Night Football* announcer was the head coach of the Oakland Raiders when the first *MNF* broadcast took place in 1970.

☐ **a.** John Madden
☐ **b.** Al Michaels
☐ **c.** Don Meredith
☐ **d.** Dennis Miller

36. Fact or Fiction: Sylvester Stallone discovered Mr. T while competing in a "World's Toughest Bouncer" competition.

☐ **a.** Fact
☐ **b.** Fiction

37. Patrick Warburton, who voices Joe on *Family Guy*, was also a regular on *Seinfeld* playing which character?

☐ **a.** J. Peterman
☐ **b.** Kenny Bania
☐ **c.** David Puddy
☐ **d.** Jackie Chiles

38. Of all the television events in U.S. history, this had the largest audience with over 50 million viewers watching in 60 percent of households.

☐ **a.** Super Bowl XLII (Patriots/Giants), 2007
☐ **b.** *Mash* series finale, 1983
☐ **c.** *Cheers* series finale, 1993
☐ **d.** *Dallas* "Who Shot J.R.?" episode, 1980

39. This famous actor left *Gunsmoke* to tackle a serious movie career. Men (and women) everywhere were grateful.

☐ **a.** John Wayne
☐ **b.** Clint Eastwood

☐ **c.** Burt Reynolds
☐ **d.** Michael Landon

40. MacGyver, the mulleted main character on—y'know—
MacGyver, always carried this with him.

☐ **a.** Swiss army knife
☐ **b.** Paper clip
☐ **c.** Zippo
☐ **d.** Fishing line

41. Fact or Fiction: The introduction to the first episode of *Gunsmoke* was voiced by John Wayne.

☐ **a.** Fact
☐ **b.** Fiction

True Story
The first couple to be shown together in bed on prime
time TV were Fred and Wilma Flintstone.

42. Which of these nicknames was not used in reference to
James Rockford in *The Rockford Files?*

☐ **a.** Sonny
☐ **b.** Rockfish
☐ **c.** Jimbo
☐ **d.** Rocket Man

43. Fact or Fiction: Rob Reiner guest-starred on an episode of
The Rockford Files without his hairpiece from *All in the Family*, so viewers would differentiate the two characters.

☐ **a.** Fact
☐ **b.** Fiction

44. Which of these actors was not in both the TV and film versions of *M*A*S*H*?

☐ **a.** Gary Burghoff
☐ **b.** G. Wood
☐ **c.** Timothy Brown
☐ **d.** Alan Alda

45. A teddy bear seen on *M*A*S*H* was sold at auction in 2005 for $11,800. The teddy bear belonged to which character on the show?

☐ **a.** Hawkeye
☐ **b.** Max Klinger
☐ **c.** Radar
☐ **d.** Hot Lips Houlihan

46. What band can we thank for *South Park*'s wicked theme?

☐ **a.** Rusted Root
☐ **b.** Pantara
☐ **c.** Primus
☐ **d.** Lynyrd Skynyrd

47. On *The Sopranos*, the fellas spend a long time hanging out in their offices in the back of this strip club.

☐ **a.** The Foxy Roxy
☐ **b.** The Doll House
☐ **c.** The Bada Bing
☐ **d.** Girls Next Door

48. What was the name of the clueless Nazi camp commander on *Hogan's Heroes*?

☐ **a.** Sgt. Schultz
☐ **b.** Col. Klink

☐ **c.** Corp. Newkirk
☐ **d.** Col. Von Luger

Classic Quote

"Television! Teacher, mother, secret lover."

—HOMER SIMPSON, *THE SIMPSONS*

49. This actor had major roles on both *Seinfeld* and *The King of Queens*.

☐ **a.** Jerry Stiller
☐ **b.** Kevin James
☐ **c.** Doug Heffernan
☐ **d.** Wayne Knight

50. Which one is blonde?

☐ **a.** Beavis
☐ **b.** Butt-head

51. This actor played the Beaver on *Leave It to Beaver*.

☐ **a.** Ron Howard
☐ **b.** Jerry Mathers
☐ **c.** Jay North
☐ **d.** Mel Gibson

52. One of the greatest questions ever asked on TV—"Do you believe in miracles!?"—was broadcast by this legend.

☐ **a.** Howard Cosell
☐ **b.** Al Michaels
☐ **c.** Bob Costas
☐ **d.** Pat Summerall

53. This classic sci-fi/horror series featured the famous episode "Time Enough at Last," starring Burgess Meredith.

☐ **a.** *Alfred Hitchcock Presents*
☐ **b.** *The Twilight Zone*
☐ **c.** *The Outer Limits*
☐ **d.** *Tales from the Darkside*

54. What was the name of Richie and Joanie Cunningham's older brother who simply disappeared after the first season of *Happy Days*?

☐ **a.** Wes
☐ **b.** Mitch
☐ **c.** Chuck
☐ **d.** Larry

55. All right, this is an easy one. Who shot J.R.?

☐ **a.** Bobby Ewing
☐ **b.** Ray Krebbs
☐ **c.** Audrey Landers
☐ **d.** Kristin Shepard

56. *The Honeymooners* lasted for how many seasons?

☐ **a.** 1
☐ **b.** 2
☐ **c.** 3
☐ **d.** 4

True Story
By the time American children reach age fourteen, on an average they have seen around 11,000 murders on television.

57. Det. Stanley Wojciehowicz was a classic character on what cop show?

☐ **a.** *Crime Story*
☐ **b.** *Barney Miller*
☐ **c.** *Miami Vice*
☐ **d.** *Starsky & Hutch*

58. Sanford and Son's salvage joint—both their home and their business—was located in what California neighborhood?

☐ **a.** Compton
☐ **b.** Venice Beach
☐ **c.** Watts
☐ **d.** Englewood

59. The classic cop line "Book 'em, Dano" comes from which show?

☐ **a.** *Hawaii 5-0*
☐ **b.** *Dragnet*
☐ **c.** *CHiPs*
☐ **d.** *S.W.A.T.*

60. Who loves ya, baby?

☐ **a.** Kojak
☐ **b.** Columbo
☐ **c.** Sipowicz
☐ **d.** Crocket

61. How does Buster Bluth lose his hand?

☐ **a.** Lucille
☐ **b.** Loose Seal
☐ **c.** Lucille Two
☐ **d.** Carl Weathers

62. *Gunsmoke* was on the air for how many years?

☐ **a.** Ten
☐ **b.** Fifteen
☐ **c.** Twenty
☐ **d.** Twenty-five

63. We all loved Suzanne Somer's buxom Chrissy on *Three's Company*. What was Chrissy short for?

☐ **a.** Christina
☐ **b.** Christmas
☐ **c.** Christopher
☐ **d.** Christy-Lou

> **Did You Know?** The first American TVs were produced in 1938. Big surprise: they were an instant hit.

64. *Married with Children*'s Al Bundy makes a living doing this miserable job.

☐ **a.** Mechanic
☐ **b.** TV repairman
☐ **c.** Shoe salesman
☐ **d.** Gigolo

65. What is MacGyver's first name?

☐ **a.** Angus
☐ **b.** Frederick
☐ **c.** Russell
☐ **d.** Maxwell

66. What does ALF stand for?

☐ **a.** Alien Life Form
☐ **b.** A Lot Furry

☐ **c.** Attacking Leftover Food
☐ **d.** Ally's Little Friend

67. This is the name of the Dukes of Hazzard's car.

☐ **a.** Mason Dixon
☐ **b.** General Lee
☐ **c.** Stars and Stripes
☐ **d.** The Rebel Ranger

68. *Mission Impossible* follows the activities of this group.

☐ **a.** IMF
☐ **b.** Eh7
☐ **c.** MI6
☐ **d.** CAC

69. What was the name of Sonny's pet alligator on *Miami Vice*?

☐ **a.** Elvis
☐ **b.** Cole
☐ **c.** Bitey
☐ **d.** Marilyn

70. What did KITT stand for?

☐ **a.** Kunning Intuitive Tech Tronic
☐ **b.** Knight Industries Tech Twelve
☐ **c.** Karmotive Industrial Triple Threat
☐ **d.** Knight Industries Two Thousand

71. On *Perfect Strangers*, Balki Bartokomous did this for a living when he lived in Mypos.

☐ **a.** Sheep rancher
☐ **b.** Alligator wrestler
☐ **c.** Nerf herder
☐ **d.** Goose catcher

Classic Quote

"Television is chewing gum for the eyes."

—FRANK LLOYD WRIGHT, ARCHITECT

72. What '80s pro wrestler was turned into a G.I. Joe action figure?

- ☐ **a.** The Ram
- ☐ **b.** Sgt. Slaughter
- ☐ **c.** Hulk Hogan
- ☐ **d.** The Iron Sheik

73. The Simpsons live in Springfield, of course. But what neighboring town is a bitter rival?

- ☐ **a.** Shelbyville
- ☐ **b.** Ogdenville
- ☐ **c.** North Haverbrook
- ☐ **d.** Brockway

74. Fact or Fiction: Charles Manson auditioned for the Monkees.

- ☐ **a.** Fact
- ☐ **b.** Fiction

75. In 1981, this became the first video to air on MTV.

- ☐ **a.** "Video Killed the Radio Star" by the Buggles
- ☐ **b.** "Hold on Loosely" by .38 Special
- ☐ **c.** "In the Air Tonight" by Phil Collins
- ☐ **d.** "You Better Run" by Pat Benatar

76. Who was the announcer on *The Price Is Right* who famously asked contestants to "Come on down!"?

- ☐ **a.** Rod Roddy
- ☐ **b.** Bob Barker

☐ **c.** Roddy Piper
☐ **d.** Bob Vila

77. Clint Eastwood got his big break playing Rowdy Yates on what TV Western?

☐ **a.** *Have Gun, Will Travel*
☐ **b.** *Gunsmoke*
☐ **c.** *Rawhide*
☐ **d.** *Wagon Train*

78. Slime was introduced on which Nickelodeon show?

☐ **a.** *Gack!*
☐ **b.** *You Can't Do That on Television*
☐ **c.** *Double Dare*
☐ **d.** *Wild and Crazy Kids*

79. Hulk Hogan starred in this 1993 action-adventure show about two mercs with a crazy badass boat.

☐ **a.** *Thunder in Paradise*
☐ **b.** *Tiger and Cobra*
☐ **c.** *The N.W.O.*
☐ **d.** *Thunder and Lightning*

Classic Quote
"Did you ever think about life as a metaphor for television?"

—CHUCK PALAHNIUK, AUTHOR

80. The first major league baseball game was broadcast on television in what year?

☐ **a.** 1934
☐ **b.** 1939
☐ **c.** 1941
☐ **d.** 1944

Did You Know? Candice Bergen was the first female *SNL* host.

81. This late-night television icon hosted *The Tonight Show* for thirty years.

☐ **a.** David Letterman
☐ **b.** Steve Allen
☐ **c.** Johnny Carson
☐ **d.** Jay Leno

82. David Letterman got his start on TV doing what?

☐ **a.** Weather
☐ **b.** Sports
☐ **c.** Investigative Journalism
☐ **d.** Sgt. Dave's Spotlight on Local Lovers

83. This actress was a cheerleader for the San Francisco 49ers long before she was one of TV's *Desperate Housewives*.

☐ **a.** Sofia Vergara
☐ **b.** Teri Hatcher
☐ **c.** Eva Longoria
☐ **d.** Nicollette Sheridan

84. Who was the first host of *Saturday Night Live*?

☐ **a.** Steve Martin
☐ **b.** George Carlin

☐ **c.** Bill Murray
☐ **d.** Joan Rivers

85. What TV cop drove suspects crazy with the trademark line, "Just one more thing. . . ."?

☐ **a.** Columbo
☐ **b.** Kojak
☐ **c.** Jessica Fletcher
☐ **d.** Starsky

86. In what year was cigarette advertising banned from television?

☐ **a.** 1971
☐ **b.** 1974
☐ **c.** 1977
☐ **d.** 1982

True Story
Franklin D. Roosevelt was the first president to appear on television. He was shown at opening ceremonies of the New York World's Fair in 1939.

87. The first televised presidential debate occurred on September 26, 1960, and took place between these two candidates.

☐ **a.** Lyndon B. Johnson and Richard Nixon
☐ **b.** John F. Kennedy and Richard Nixon
☐ **c.** Dwight Eisenhower and John F. Kennedy
☐ **d.** Lyndon B. Johnson and Hubert Humphrey

88. Nearly every *Seinfeld* episode contains an image or reference to this superhero.

- [ ] **a.** Mr. Fantastic
- [ ] **b.** Wonder Woman
- [ ] **c.** Superman
- [ ] **d.** Batman

89. This phrase adorns a UFO poster on the wall of Fox Mulder's office in *The X-Files.*

- [ ] **a.** We Shall Overcome
- [ ] **b.** Trust No One
- [ ] **c.** Believe
- [ ] **d.** The Truth Is Out There

90. On *The Wire*, who got Stringer Bell in the end?

- [ ] **a.** Avon and Omar
- [ ] **b.** Omar and Brother Mouzone
- [ ] **c.** Brother Mouzone and Avon
- [ ] **d.** Bunk and Jimmy

91. This man owned the Gem Theater, the saloon and brothel on the HBO series *Deadwood*. It also happened to exist in real life.

- [ ] **a.** George Hurst
- [ ] **b.** E.B. Farnum
- [ ] **c.** Al Swearengen
- [ ] **d.** Seth Bullock

92. This pop star and actress got her start as one of the Fly Girls on *In Living Color*.

- [ ] **a.** Jennifer Lopez
- [ ] **b.** Mariah Carey
- [ ] **c.** Alicia
- [ ] **d.** Brandy

93. Which one is Ren—the cat or the dog?

☐ **a.** Cat
☐ **b.** Dog

94. If you grew up in the '90s, you invariably ended up watching *Beverly Hills 90210*. It was impossible not to! Where the did the crew hang out?

☐ **a.** The Max
☐ **b.** Arnold's
☐ **c.** The Double R
☐ **d.** The Peach Pit

> **Did You Know?** *Leave It to Beaver* was the first TV program to show a toilet.

95. In the classic *Seinfeld* episode "The Contest," what was the contest all about?

☐ **a.** Masturbation
☐ **b.** BIrth control
☐ **c.** Oral sex
☐ **d.** Dancing

96. This was the name of the butler on *The Fresh Prince of Bel-Air*.

☐ **a.** Geoffrey
☐ **b.** Jeeves
☐ **c.** Carlton
☐ **d.** Philip

97. All right, Homer. Tell us, who shot Mr. Burns?

- ☐ **a.** Baby Gerald
- ☐ **b.** Lisa
- ☐ **c.** Maggie
- ☐ **d.** Grandpa Simpson

98. How did Webster get from the upper level of the house to the lower level?

- ☐ **a.** Hidden staircase
- ☐ **b.** Fire pole
- ☐ **c.** Ladder
- ☐ **d.** Dumbwaiter

99. On *Battlestar Galactica*, this man betrays the human race to help the Cylons.

- ☐ **a.** John Colicos
- ☐ **b.** Boomer
- ☐ **c.** Baltar
- ☐ **d.** Starbuck

100. On *Diff'rent Strokes*, Arnold had a pet named Abraham. What was it?

- ☐ **a.** Goldfish
- ☐ **b.** Dog
- ☐ **c.** Rooster
- ☐ **d.** Lizard

ANSWER KEY
CHAPTER 6. TELEVISION: THE BOOB TUBE

1. a.

2. b.

3. a.

4. d. Red, of course.

5. a.

6. b.

7. d.

8. d.

9. c.

10. c.

11. a.

12. d. Just keeps going, and going, and going . . . .

13. a.

14. c.

15. d.

16. b.

17. d.

18. a.

19. b.

20. b. Though he's hosted like a billion times.

21. c.

22. c.

23. a.

24. d.

25. d.

26. b.

27. d.

28. d.

29. a.

30. a.

31. a. Or as we call it, Bob Barker's Crazy Sexual Harassment Zone.

32. c.

33. d. And yeah—that doesn't make a whole lot of sense to us either.

34. b.

35. a.

36. a. It landed him the role of Clubber Lang in *Rocky II*. The rest, as they say, is history.

37. c.

38. b.

39. c.

40. a.

41. a.

42. d.

43. a.

44. d.

45. c.

46. c.

47. c. Not a bad working environment.

48. b.

49. a.

50. a.

51. b.

52. b. He was a young buck when he made the famous call.

53. b.

54. c.

55. d.

56. a. But it was a helluva season—and it was thirty-nine episodes long!

57. b.

58. c.

59. a.

60. a.

61. b.

62. c.

63. b.

64. c.

65. a.

66. a.

67. b.

68. a. IMF stands for Impossible Mission Force. Believe it or not, not a real thing!

69. a.

70. d.

71. a.

72. b.

73. a.

74. b. This rumor has been floating around for years, but there's nothing to it.

75. a.

76. a.

77. c.

78. b.

79. a.

80. b. The game was played between the Brooklyn Dodgers and the Cincinnati Reds.

81. c.

82. a.

83. b.

84. b.

85. a.

86. a. The law was passed in 1970, but didn't go into effect until 1971.

87. b.

88. c.

89. d.

90. b.

91. c.

92. a.

93. b.

94. d.

95. a.

96. a.

97. c.

98. d.

99. c. On both the original and the reimagining.

100. a.

SCORE!

81–100: Jack Bauer, you're a lean, mean, trivia torturin' machine.

61–80: What up, Walker, Texas Ranger? Nice roundhouse kick you got there.

41–60: You're like an episode of *Two and a Half Men*. Just sorta blah.

21–40: Time to put you in reruns.

0–20: Do you know the theme song to *Care Bears*? You do, don't you? We knew it!

CHAPTER 7

TRANSPORTATION: PLANES, TRAINS, AND AUTOMOBILES

Don't worry, this section is about more than just seeing if you know how to change a tire. Guys like things that are fast and loud, like jumbo jets, Harleys, and Apache attack choppers. But do you actualy know anything about them? Time to find out. You're behind the wheel—let's see what you've got.

1. This type of transmission will give you a 10 percent mileage boost.

   ☐ **a.** Manual
   ☐ **b.** Automatic

2. This company started out manufacturing airplanes before they moved onto automobiles.

   ☐ **a.** Mercedes-Benz
   ☐ **b.** Saab
   ☐ **c.** Rolls-Royce
   ☐ **d.** Porsche

3. Any real man should know how to change a tire. Not that we're judging. Match the action with the order it should be done (all while showing off your skills to that hot little number riding shotgun).

   ☐ **i.** Jack up the car   **a.** Sixth
   ☐ **ii.** Take lug nuts off   **b.** Fifth
   ☐ **iii.** Pull the tire off   **c.** First
   ☐ **iv.** Have the girl do it   **d.** Second
   ☐ **v.** Loosen lug nuts   **e.** Third
   ☐ **vi.** Lower the car   **f.** Seventh
   ☐ **vii.** Put lug nuts on   **g.** Never
   ☐ **viii.** Tighten lug nuts   **h.** Fourth

4. The alternator on your car does what?

   ☐ **a.** Charges your battery
   ☐ **b.** Cleans coolant for the A/C
   ☐ **c.** Stabilizes the brakes
   ☐ **d.** Controls the power steering

5. Match the classic American muscle car with its manufacturer. All or nothing on the points here, so think hard!

☐ **i.** Mustang   **a.** Oldsmobile
☐ **ii.** 442   **b.** Mercury
☐ **iii.** Roadrunner   **c.** Ford
☐ **iv.** GTO   **d.** Plymouth
☐ **v.** Challenger   **e.** Buick
☐ **vi.** Nova   **f.** Pontiac
☐ **vii.** GSX   **g.** Chevrolet
☐ **viii.** Cougar   **h.** Dodge

6. Fact or Fiction: The oil in your car must be changed every 3,000 miles.

☐ **a.** Fact
☐ **b.** Fiction

7. Some fighter jets can go high enough to see the curvature of the Earth. Pretty crazy right? What altitude (in feet) can a Russian Mig-29 Fighter jet fly?

☐ **a.** 25,250
☐ **b.** 42,000
☐ **c.** 59,058
☐ **d.** 80,740

8. The world's fastest high-speed train debuted in Shanghai in 2004. It moves at a max of 268 MPH. What propels this train?

☐ **a.** Coal
☐ **b.** Diesel engine
☐ **c.** Nuclear reactor
☐ **d.** Magnetic levitation

9. Fact or Fiction: Amtrak is owned and run by the federal government.

   ☐ **a.** Fact
   ☐ **b.** Fiction

10. This ocean-dwelling creature was the name of an extremely popular model of Corvette.

    ☐ **a.** Shark
    ☐ **b.** Stingray
    ☐ **c.** Squid
    ☐ **d.** Marlin

11. This car, produced by Ford, ended up being the title of a Clint Eastwood film.

    ☐ **a.** Thunderbird
    ☐ **b.** Explorer
    ☐ **c.** Mustang
    ☐ **d.** Gran Torino

12. The first stock car race drivers were actually outlaws who honed their skills behind the wheel doing this.

    ☐ **a.** Robbing banks
    ☐ **b.** Bootlegging
    ☐ **c.** Driving a getaway car
    ☐ **d.** Dealing drugs

13. For the average guy, changing a tire is a time-consuming pain in the ass, especially if you're stuck trying to do it on the side of the road. But NASCAR pit crews are so adept at changing tires, it only takes them:

- ☐ **a.** Thirteen seconds
- ☐ **b.** Eighteen seconds
- ☐ **c.** Twenty-three seconds
- ☐ **d.** Thirty-five seconds

14. Many people have a fear of flying. But really, just how justified is that fear? What are the odds of being involved in a fatal airplane crash, even if you're flying with one of the twenty-five worst airlines (as far as crash track record)?

- ☐ **a.** 1 in 35,000
- ☐ **b.** 1 in 244,679
- ☐ **c.** 1 in 843,744
- ☐ **d.** 1 in 4.3 million

15. The term DOHC is common on car engines these days. Do you know what it stands for?

- ☐ **a.** Double Oil, Hot Coolant
- ☐ **b.** Double Overhead Cam
- ☐ **c.** Dual Over Hand Clutches
- ☐ **d.** Downshift on Highway Control

16. Law enforcement agencies have many different cars in their fleets, but for the last thirty years, this car has pretty much been *the* cop car.

- ☐ **a.** Chevy Caprice
- ☐ **b.** Ford Crown Victoria
- ☐ **c.** Dodge Durango
- ☐ **d.** Toyota Camry

17. The Buick Grand National was a huge hit when it came on the scene in the '80s with its turbocharged engine in this configuration.

☐ **a.** V10
☐ **b.** V8
☐ **c.** V6
☐ **d.** 4-cylinder

18. This is the preferred tank of the U.S. Army; some variant has been in use since 1978.

☐ **a.** M1 Abrams
☐ **b.** M46
☐ **c.** Sherman
☐ **d.** M26

19. If you want to impress the ladies with that ¼-mile time, you better make sure your car has some traction. You'll need to equip your car with tires with just a little tread and lots of grip. These are known as what?

☐ **a.** Mudders
☐ **b.** Slicks
☐ **c.** Grippers
☐ **d.** No Treads

20. Fact or Fiction: The movie *Silver Streak* was shot along actual Amtrak train routes.

☐ **a.** Fact
☐ **b.** Fiction

21. Some of the largest vehicles on Earth are aircraft carriers, and the U.S. Navy employs the biggest of the big boys with its Nimitz class. What type of aircraft is most common on these floating fortresses?

☐ **a.** F-22 Raptor
☐ **b.** F-14 Tomcat
☐ **c.** F-18 Super Hornet
☐ **d.** F-16 Fighting Falcon

22. Damn near every episode of *The Rockford Files* featured a balls-to-the-wall car chase. What kind of car was Rockford tooling around in in all those episodes?

☐ **a.** Chevrolet Camaro
☐ **b.** Pontiac Firebird
☐ **c.** Chevrolet Corvette
☐ **d.** Pontiac GTO

23. Match the Bond car with the Bond movie it starred in.

☐ **i.** Aston Martin DB5   **a.** *Goldfinger*
☐ **ii.** Ford Mustang Mach 1   **b.** *The Spy Who Loved Me*
☐ **iii.** AMC Hornet   **c.** *Goldeneye*
☐ **iv.** Lotus Esprit   **d.** *The Man with the Golden Gun*
☐ **v.** BMW Z3   **e.** *Diamonds Are Forever*

24. What was the name of the Wright Brothers' first aircraft?

☐ **a.** Flyer
☐ **b.** Floater
☐ **c.** Glider
☐ **d.** Air Time

True Story
A first-class ticket on the *Titanic* cost roughly $100,000 when adjusted for inflation.

25. The Wright Brothers' first flight took place where?

☐ **a.** Chattanooga, Tennessee
☐ **b.** Jacksonville, Florida
☐ **c.** Black Hawk, Colorado
☐ **d.** Kitty Hawk, North Carolina

26. The first NASCAR race took place in what year?

☐ **a.** 1937
☐ **b.** 1949
☐ **c.** 1953
☐ **d.** 1967

27. Everyone knows the legend of Evel Knievel, but do you know his real name?

☐ **a.** Robert Mark Knievel
☐ **b.** Joseph Harris Knievel
☐ **c.** Robert Craig Knievel
☐ **d.** Thomas John Knievel

28. The DeLorean went from infamous to famous after *Back to the Future*. What material was the car made from?

☐ **a.** Stainless steel
☐ **b.** Aluminum
☐ **c.** Graphite
☐ **d.** Iron

29. Bonnie and Clyde were famously ambushed and gunned down in this type of car?

☐ **a.** 1932 Pontiac 8
☐ **b.** 1930 Buick Series 40 Phaeton
☐ **c.** 1934 Ford V8
☐ **d.** 1931 Studebaker 6

30. This car may have been one of the best selling cars of the '70s, but it was a PR disaster. Why? Because it had one tiny little problem: a habit of exploding when it got rear-ended.

☐ **a.** Ford Pinto
☐ **b.** Chevrolet Chevette
☐ **c.** AMC Gremlin
☐ **d.** AMC Pacer

31. This car was a piece of junk, but it sold boatloads. Why? Because it was the cheapest car of the 1980s.

☐ **a.** Nova
☐ **b.** Yugo
☐ **c.** Escort
☐ **d.** Taurus

32. What kind of car does Mad Max drive in *The Road Warrior*?

☐ **a.** El Camino
☐ **b.** Ford Falcon
☐ **c.** Pontiac Catalina
☐ **d.** Ford Fairlane

True Story
A Boeing 747 has six million parts—and half of them are fasteners.

33. Pilot Sully Sullenberger is famous for what?

☐ **a.** Taking out more than twenty-five planes in Vietnam
☐ **b.** Being the first to enter outer space
☐ **c.** Landing a plane on the Hudson River
☐ **d.** First pilot to break the sound barrier

34. No color/car combination is as intertwined as pink and Cadillac. There's even a song called "Pink Cadillac"! Which artist sings that little diddy?

☐ **a.** Bruce Springsteen
☐ **b.** Billy Joel
☐ **c.** John Mellencamp
☐ **d.** Rick Springfield

35. Fact or Fiction: A red car will cost you a higher insurance premium.

☐ **a.** Fact
☐ **b.** Fiction

36. Fact or Fiction: You are more likely to get pulled over driving a red car.

☐ **a.** Fact
☐ **b.** Fiction

37. In *American Graffiti*, what car was Bob Falfa (played by a young Harrison Ford) cruising around in?

☐ **a.** '32 Ford Coupe
☐ **b.** '55 Chevy
☐ **c.** '56 T-Bird
☐ **d.** '51 Mercury

38. This is the world's fastest production car at 267 MPH . . . and it could be yours for just $2,400,000!

☐ **a.** Saleen S7 Twin Turbo
☐ **b.** McLaren F1
☐ **c.** Ferrari Enzo
☐ **d.** Bugatti Veyron Super Sport

39. Sir Mix-a-Lot's classic car song "My Hooptie" is about the car he's forced to drive while his Benz in the shop. What type of car is it?

- ☐ **a.** '69 Buick
- ☐ **b.** BMW
- ☐ **c.** Porsche
- ☐ **d.** '75 Vette

40. What type of cars are used in both the original and remake versions of *The Italian Job*?

- ☐ **a.** Beetle
- ☐ **b.** Porsche
- ☐ **c.** Charger
- ☐ **d.** Mini

> **Did You Know?** The Wright Brothers' first flight was shorter than the wingspan of a B-52 bomber.

41. Who sings the ultra '80s song "Cars"?

- ☐ **a.** The Cars
- ☐ **b.** Gary Numan
- ☐ **c.** A Flock of Seagulls
- ☐ **d.** Corey Hart

42. The Beatles' song "Drive My Car" appeared on which album?

- ☐ **a.** *Please, Please Me*
- ☐ **b.** *Sgt. Pepper's Lonely Hearts Club Band*
- ☐ **c.** *Help!*
- ☐ **d.** *Rubber Soul*

43. What best describes a "pony" car?

  ☐ **a.** A compact, sporty car that's affordable
  ☐ **b.** An expensive sports car, the term implying that you'll have to "pony" up a lot of dough to buy one
  ☐ **c.** Any line of car named after a horse—Mustang, for example
  ☐ **d.** Any car that's been heavily modified by its owner

44. This car was the first to be mass-produced—and it changed history.

  ☐ **a.** Model A
  ☐ **b.** Model T
  ☐ **c.** Daimler
  ☐ **d.** Duesenberg

45. SoCal cops Starsky and Hutch drove this kind of car.

  ☐ **a.** Plymouth Barracuda
  ☐ **b.** Ford Gran Torino
  ☐ **c.** Pontiac Firebird
  ☐ **d.** AMC Javelin

46. Manfred von Richthofen, better known as the Red Baron, had how many air combat victories during World War I?

  ☐ **a.** Forty
  ☐ **b.** Sixty
  ☐ **c.** Eighty
  ☐ **d.** One hundred

47. The first modern-style motorcycle was built by German inventor Gottlieb Daimler in what year?

  ☐ **a.** 1865
  ☐ **b.** 1885
  ☐ **c.** 1905
  ☐ **d.** 1925

48. On *CHiPs*, motorcycle cops Ponch and Jon patrolled the California highway on what brand of bike?

☐ **a.** Kawasaki
☐ **b.** Harley-Davidson
☐ **c.** Honda
☐ **d.** Ducati

Top 5 List

Our five favorite guy flicks

The Road Warrior
The French Connection
To Live and Die in L.A.
The Driver
The Blues Brothers

49. Turn signals become standard on cars in which decade?

☐ **a.** 1920s
☐ **b.** 1930s
☐ **c.** 1940s
☐ **d.** 1950s

50. Fact or Fiction: There are more cars than people in Los Angeles.

☐ **a.** Fact
☐ **b.** Fiction

51. "Eleanor" in *Gone in 60 Seconds* (the Nic Cage version) is what kind of car?

☐ **a.** 1998 Porsche 911 Turbo
☐ **b.** 2000 Cadillac Escalade EXT
☐ **c.** 1967 Mustang GT 500
☐ **d.** 1963 Ferrari 250 GT

52. Fact or Fiction. The "Eleanor" car from the original 1974 version of the film was a Mustang.

- [ ] **a.** Fact
- [ ] **b.** Fiction

53. This motorcycle maker produces models such as "Vegas" and "Kingpin."

- [ ] **a.** Harley-Davidson
- [ ] **b.** Triumph
- [ ] **c.** Victory
- [ ] **d.** Indian

54. What year marked the debut of the Corvette?

- [ ] **a.** 1949
- [ ] **b.** 1953
- [ ] **c.** 1961
- [ ] **d.** 1970

55. Ray Harroun gained notoriety for this little-seen device on his car in 1911 during the inaugural Indianapolis 500.

- [ ] **a.** Rubber tires
- [ ] **b.** V8 engine
- [ ] **c.** Rearview mirror
- [ ] **d.** Convertible top

Classic Quote

"Rail travel at high speed is not possible because passengers, unable to breathe, would die of asphyxia."

—DR. DIONYSYS LARDER (1793–1859)

56. This car company was the first to offer turn signals as a standard feature.

☐ **a.** Ford
☐ **b.** Buick
☐ **c.** Chevrolet
☐ **d.** Chrysler

57. The first cars boasting seatbelts came out in what year?

☐ **a.** 1935
☐ **b.** 1944
☐ **c.** 1958
☐ **d.** 1961

58. Rear seatbelts became standard on American cars in what year?

☐ **a.** 1959
☐ **b.** 1968
☐ **c.** 1971
☐ **d.** 1980

59. The first ever supplemental air bag was offered in 1981 by what auto maker?

☐ **a.** Mercedes
☐ **b.** BMW
☐ **c.** Audi
☐ **d.** Chevrolet

60. The "Blue Angels" are part of which branch of the military?

☐ **a.** Army
☐ **b.** Air Force
☐ **c.** Navy
☐ **d.** Marines

61. Like most people, you probably aren't a fan of the insurance policies you have to pay on your car. The car insurance racket started with the first policy sold in Dayton, Ohio, in what year?

☐ **a.** 1897
☐ **b.** 1902
☐ **c.** 1913
☐ **d.** 1927

62. Remember these words when you're on a plane—they dictate when to anticipate danger and stay alert.

☐ **a.** Early and often
☐ **b.** Plus three minus eight
☐ **c.** Height of flight
☐ **d.** Mile-high sleeping guy

63. Fact or Fiction: Many people who don't survive plane crashes die because they are trying to take their carry-on luggage.

☐ **a.** Fact
☐ **b.** Fiction

64. During a plane crash, you have roughly how long to exit the plane before it's too late?

☐ **a.** Twenty-five seconds
☐ **b.** Ninety seconds
☐ **c.** Two minutes
☐ **d.** Four minutes, thirty seconds

65. An airplane "black box" flight recorder is what color?

☐ **a.** Black
☐ **b.** Red
☐ **c.** Orange
☐ **d.** Blue

True Story
Henry Winkler—a.k.a. The Fonz—was terrified of
motorcycles, and never actually rode one!

66. Fact or Fiction: You must have 20/20 vision without the aid of
corrective lenses in order to become an airline pilot.

☐ **a.** Fact
☐ **b.** Fiction

67. In the movie *Airplane*, what does the translation under the
"fasten your seatbelts" sign say?

☐ **a.** Ajustarse los cinturones de seguridad
☐ **b.** Putana da seatbeltz
☐ **c.** Boucle jusqu'à
☐ **d.** Doitta nowisay

68. In what year did the Hindenburg crash?

☐ **a.** 1916
☐ **b.** 1923
☐ **c.** 1937
☐ **d.** 1949

69. In train terms, what is a roundhouse?

☐ **a.** The way Chuck Norris beats up trains
☐ **b.** A place to pick up and drop off passengers
☐ **c.** A place to make train repairs
☐ **d.** An intersection of railways

70. Trains use what material to help climb steeper grades?

☐ **a.** Water
☐ **b.** Sand
☐ **c.** Tree sap
☐ **d.** Salt

71. Antifreeze goes into what part of your car?

☐ **a.** Engine
☐ **b.** A/C
☐ **c.** Radiator
☐ **d.** Battery

True Story
It takes an airbag roughly forty milliseconds to deploy.

72. The song "Night Train" is by what artist?

☐ **a.** Steve Winwood
☐ **b.** Bob Seger
☐ **c.** Fleetwood Mac
☐ **d.** Corey Hart

73. "Midnight Train to Georgia" is a classic from this group.

☐ **a.** Junior Walker and the All Stars
☐ **b.** Gladys Knight and the Pips
☐ **c.** The Marvelettes
☐ **d.** Jimmy Ruffin

Top 5 List

Our five favorite fictional vehicles:	Optimus Prime (obviously #1)
	The Batmobile
	KITT
	The Mystery Machine
	Mad Max's Interceptor

74. This is the type of car Janis Joplin asks the Lord to buy her.

☐ **a.** Jaguar
☐ **b.** Chevy
☐ **c.** Mercedes-Benz
☐ **d.** Chrysler

75. Which band had a hit with their song "Long Train Running"?

- [ ] **a.** Allman Brothers
- [ ] **b.** The Everly Brothers
- [ ] **c.** Righteous Brothers
- [ ] **d.** Doobie Brothers

76. The Beach Boys sang about a Chevy with this engine?

- [ ] **a.** 454
- [ ] **b.** 409
- [ ] **c.** 350
- [ ] **d.** 396

77. If you want to listen to the song "Red Barchetta" (about a futuristic car chase) just grab this band's *Moving Pictures* album.

- [ ] **a.** Van Halen
- [ ] **b.** Styx
- [ ] **c.** Rush
- [ ] **d.** Foreigner

78. When determining the side of a boat relative to the wind, what terms are used?

- [ ] **a.** Port/Starboard
- [ ] **b.** Windward/Leeward
- [ ] **c.** Aft/Bow
- [ ] **d.** None of these

Classic Quote
"God Forgives. Outlaws Don't."
—THE OUTLAWS MOTORCYCLE GANG

79. What is the name of a two-mast sailing vessel with a taller aft mast than forward mast?

☐ **a.** Yawl
☐ **b.** Schooner
☐ **c.** Ketch
☐ **d.** Sunfish

80. On a boat, the small pennant used to determine wind direction is known as a what?

☐ **a.** Burgee
☐ **b.** Compass
☐ **c.** Diceometer
☐ **d.** Sock

81. What does the RMS in RMS *Titanic* stand for?

☐ **a.** Royal Merchant Ship
☐ **b.** Ready More Shrimp
☐ **c.** Royal Mail Steamer
☐ **d.** Rough Measured Seas

Did You Know? In the entire state of Ohio in 1895, there were only two cars on the road—and they crashed into each other.

82. Iberia is the national airline for what country?

☐ **a.** England
☐ **b.** Libya
☐ **c.** Spain
☐ **d.** Portugal

83. Christopher Cockerell is known as the inventor of what flat-out awesome mode of transportation?

☐ **a.** Hovercraft
☐ **b.** Helicopter
☐ **c.** Jetpack
☐ **d.** Subway

84. Chili Palmer, the loan shark from Miami, shocks the LA crowd with this car in *Get Shorty*.

☐ **a.** 1989 Chevy Nova
☐ **b.** 1994 Oldsmobile Silhouette
☐ **c.** 1993 Eagle Talon
☐ **d.** 1988 Chevy Camaro

85. What make of car does Jack Cate drive in *48 Hrs?*

☐ **a.** Buick
☐ **b.** Chevy
☐ **c.** Ford
☐ **d.** Cadillac

86. What car continually gets abused by the comedic mishaps of Chris Farley in *Tommy Boy*?

☐ **a.** 1947 Buick Roadmaster
☐ **b.** 1967 Plymouth Belvedere GTX
☐ **c.** 1970 Pontiac GTO
☐ **d.** 1969 Ford Mustang

87. Wayne was known to drive around blasting "Bohemian Rhapsody" in this kind of car in *Wayne's World*.

☐ **a.** AMC Pacer
☐ **b.** Ford Pinto
☐ **c.** AMC Gremlin
☐ **d.** Chevy Nova

88. In *The Blue Brothers*, Jake and Elwood cruise around in this kind of cop car.

☐ **a.** Chevy Impala
☐ **b.** Ford Crown Victoria
☐ **c.** Dodge Monaco
☐ **d.** Plymouth Roadrunner

Classic Quote

"When we do right, nobody remembers. When we do wrong, nobody forgets."

—THE HELL'S ANGELS

89. The Duke brothers (of *Dukes of Hazzard* fame) drive what kind of car?

☐ **a.** Dodge Challenger
☐ **b.** Ford Gran Torino
☐ **c.** Mercury Cougar
☐ **d.** Plymouth Duster

90. "Greased Lightning" is what kind of car?

☐ **a.** '55 Chevy
☐ **b.** '44 Olds
☐ **c.** '48 Ford
☐ **d.** '53 Plymouth

91. The John Hughes classic *Planes, Trains and Automobiles* stars John Candy and this funny man.

☐ **a.** Robin Williams
☐ **b.** Steve Martin
☐ **c.** Bill Maher
☐ **d.** Bill Murray

92. This is the name of the P-51 Mustang flown by Chuck Yeager during WWII.

☐ **a.** Killer Bee
☐ **b.** Mustang Sally
☐ **c.** Glamorous Glennis
☐ **d.** Faithfull Shooter

93. Charles Lindbergh was flying this plane when he crossed the Atlantic.

☐ **a.** The Holy Flyer
☐ **b.** The Dakota Fang
☐ **c.** The Spirit of St. Louis
☐ **d.** The Boston Tea Party

94. Which of these men was *not* killed in a plane crash?

☐ **a.** Otis Redding
☐ **b.** Buddy Holly
☐ **c.** Thurman Munson
☐ **d.** Ty Cobb

95. The famous Orient-Express ran from Paris to what location?

☐ **a.** Istanbul
☐ **b.** Mosul
☐ **c.** Cairo
☐ **d.** Dubai

True Story
Every twenty-five seconds, a car gets stolen in America.

96. The first space shuttle was launched in what year?

☐ **a.** 1960
☐ **b.** 1974
☐ **c.** 1981
☐ **d.** 1990

97. The first jet to break the sound barrier was piloted by Chuck Yeager in what year?

☐ **a.** 1933
☐ **b.** 1947
☐ **c.** 1951
☐ **d.** 1959

98. In 1968, Dodge released what car to compete with Plymouth's hit Roadrunner?

☐ **a.** Charger
☐ **b.** Challenger
☐ **c.** Super Bee
☐ **d.** Magnum

99. The Chrysler's 426 HEMI engine is legendary among the car community. What's the engine's nickname?

☐ **a.** Tiger
☐ **b.** Elephant
☐ **c.** Puma
☐ **d.** Hippo

100. The Pontiac GTO may just be the car that started the muscle, but what does GTO stand for?

☐ **a.** Great Touring Otto
☐ **b.** Gran Turismo Omologato
☐ **c.** Grand Touring Outside
☐ **d.** Geared To Outrun

ANSWER KEY
CHAPTER 7. TRANSPORTATION: PLANES, TRAINS, AND AUTOMOBILES

1. a.

2. b.

3. i. d; ii. e; iii. h; iv. g; v. c; vi. a; vii. b; viii. f

4. a.

5. i. c; ii. a; iii. d; iv. f; v. h; vi. g; vii. e; viii. b

6. b.

7. c.

8. d.

9. a.

10. b.

11. d.

12. b.

13. a.

14. c.

15. b.

16. b.

17. c.

18. a.

19. b.

20. b. Amtrak was fearful of bad publicity so it was forced to use Canadian railways.

21. c. The fleet of F-18 Hornets is still being transitioned to F-18 Super Hornets.

22. b.

23. i. a; ii. e; iii. d; iv. b; v. c

24. a.

25. d.

26. b.

27. c.

28. a.

29. c.

30. a.

31. b.

32. b. It's not stock, but it's a Falcon.

33. c.

34. a.

35. b. Insurance companies usually don't even know the color of the car they are insuring when a quote is given.

36. b. While it is a popular urban legend, there is no evidence to support the claim.

37. b.

38. d. A man can dream, dammit.

39. a.

40. d.

41. b. Go watch the video and try and tell us you want any part of the '80s back.

42. d. Beep beep, beep beep!

43. a.

44. b.

45. b.

46. c.

47. b.

48. a.

49. b.

50. a.

51. c.

52. a.

53. c.

54. b.

55. c.

56. b.

57. c.

58. b.

59. a.

60. c.

61. a.

62. b. Be alert three minutes after takeoff and eight minutes before landing. That's when most plane crashes occur.

63. a.

64. b.

65. c.

66. b.

67. b.

68. c.

69. c.

70. b.

71. c.

72. a.

73. b.

74. c.

75. d.

76. b.

77. c.

78. b.

79. b.

80. a.

81. c. Now the "S" stands for ship, but it means the ship carries mail for the Royal Mail service.

82. c.

83. a.

84. b.

85. d.

86. b.

87. a.

88. c.

89. a. Orange, of course.

90. c.

91. b.

92. c.

93. c.

94. d.

95. a.

96. c.

97. b.

98. c.

99. b.

100. b.

SCORE!

81–100: Just go join a pit crew already. You could probably build Jay Leno's garage! (Cars included.)

61–80: Like a '69 Camaro, vintage gold.

41–60: Starting to get into sedan status here, but at least it's something decent—maybe an '80s Saab.

21–40: "Pow, pow, power wheels!"

0–20: Yugo. That's you . . . a Yugo. You should feel ashamed.

CHAPTER 8

GENDER RELATIONS: IMPRESSING THE LADIES

Nothing impresses a lady like knowing important stuff about important ladies. It's that line of thinking that resulted in this quiz. It covers the things you ought to know about the dames you say you love so much. Don't think it will be easy, either. You're gonna have to take some time to get to know this section before you have your way with it.

1. If you've ever written a paper by hand, you were certainly thankful for this 1956 invention from Bette Nesmith Graham.

   ☐ **a.** Stapler
   ☐ **b.** Liquid paper
   ☐ **c.** Ball point pen
   ☐ **d.** Erasable ink

2. Marie Curie was the first woman to do what?

   ☐ **a.** Win an Olympic gold medal
   ☐ **b.** Win a Nobel Prize
   ☐ **c.** Vote in an election
   ☐ **d.** Climb Mt. Everest

3. The Nineteenth Amendment finally gave women the right to vote. When was it ratified?

   ☐ **a.** 1894
   ☐ **b.** 1911
   ☐ **c.** 1920
   ☐ **d.** 1931

4. This woman was not only a battlefield nurse, but she was the founder of the American Red Cross.

   ☐ **a.** Betty Claiborne
   ☐ **b.** Sarah Silver
   ☐ **c.** Clara Barton
   ☐ **d.** Lizzy Borden

5. "The way I see it, if you want the rainbow, you gotta put up with the rain." This quote comes from whom?

   ☐ **a.** Emily Dickinson
   ☐ **b.** Dolly Parton
   ☐ **c.** Britney Spears
   ☐ **d.** Janis Joplin

6. Fact or Fiction: The female egg is the largest cell in the human body.

   ☐ **a.** Fact
   ☐ **b.** Fiction

7. Fact or Fiction: In most countries, the life expectancy for women is higher than for men.

   ☐ **a.** Fact
   ☐ **b.** Fiction

8. International Women's Day is held on what date each year?

   ☐ **a.** January 12th
   ☐ **b.** March 8th
   ☐ **c.** July 17th
   ☐ **d.** October 5th

> **Did You Know?** A woman named Susan Kare created many of the interface elements for the Apple Macintosh.

9. Fact or Fiction: The first woman to run for President of the United States did so shortly after women were granted the power to vote.

   ☐ **a.** Fact
   ☐ **b.** Fiction

10. Rebecca Lee Crumpler was the first black woman in the United States to receive her MD. She accomplished this feat in what year?

    ☐ **a.** 1864
    ☐ **b.** 1899
    ☐ **c.** 1914
    ☐ **d.** 1932

11. Mary Anderson patented this game-changing device in 1903—and cruisin' for babes hasn't been the same since!

☐ **a.** Headlights
☐ **b.** Windshield Wipers
☐ **c.** Rearview Mirror
☐ **d.** Seatbelts

12. Madame Curie discovered what element?

☐ **a.** Plutonium
☐ **b.** Uranium
☐ **c.** Radium
☐ **d.** Beryllium

13. Fact or Fiction: According to a poll, men shower more often than women.

☐ **a.** Fact
☐ **b.** Fiction

14. Sophia Loren's sister married the son of what famous world leader?

☐ **a.** Franklin D. Roosevelt
☐ **b.** Benito Mussolini
☐ **c.** Winston Churchill
☐ **d.** Joseph Stalin

15. What is the largest number of children one woman has ever given birth to?

☐ **a.** Twenty-one
☐ **b.** Thirty-six
☐ **c.** Forty
☐ **d.** Sixty-nine

16. When you're in the sack, you need to protect yourself. Everyone knows that. So on that topic, how many condoms are used worldwide every year?

☐ **a.** Over 240 million
☐ **b.** Over 1 billion
☐ **c.** Over 10 billion
☐ **d.** Over 100 billion

True Story
Tomb Raider's Lara Croft was originally going to be named Lara Cruz.

17. This woman won a gold medal in figure skating at the '68 Winter Olympics in Grenoble.

☐ **a.** Peggy Fleming
☐ **b.** Michelle Kwan
☐ **c.** Carol Heiss
☐ **d.** Dorothy Hamill

18. This one's for all the stamp collectors out there. (That's still a thing, right? Stamp collecting?) Match the woman on the stamp with her claim to fame.

☐ **i.** Susan B. Anthony   **a.** First woman to fly solo across the Atlantic

☐ **ii.** Juliette Gordon Low   **b.** Maker of the American flag
☐ **iii.** Betsy Ross   **c.** Women's rights activist
☐ **iv.** Amelia Earhart   **d.** Pulitzer Prize–winning author
☐ **v.** Edith Wharton   **e.** Founder of the Girl Scouts of America

19. Hattie McDaniel became the first African-American woman to win an Academy Award when she took home the Best Supporting Actress Oscar for her role in this movie.

☐ **a.** *West Side Story*
☐ **b.** *Island in the Sun*
☐ **c.** *Gone with the Wind*
☐ **d.** *Princess Tam Tam*

20. This woman famously said, "Failure is impossible."

☐ **a.** Susan B. Anthony
☐ **b.** Amelia Earhart
☐ **c.** Golda Meir
☐ **d.** Coretta Scott King

21. This brave woman was known as "the Angel of the Battlefield" for all the work she did as a nurse during the Civil War.

☐ **a.** Susan B. Anthony
☐ **b.** Ginny Ryan
☐ **c.** Clara Barton
☐ **d.** Betsy Ross

22. This was Marilyn Monroe's birth name.

☐ **a.** Norma Jeane Baker
☐ **b.** Marilyn Kennedy
☐ **c.** Susan L. Horowitz
☐ **d.** Madeline June Taylor

23. Fact or Fiction: It is impossible for a woman to get pregnant while she's on her period.

☐ **a.** Fact
☐ **b.** Fiction

24. What does the G stand for in G-Spot?

☐ **a.** Grafenberg
☐ **b.** Glandular
☐ **c.** Guberheim
☐ **d.** Goddamnit, where is this thing?

Classic Quote
"Don't compromise yourself. You are all you've got."

—JANIS JOPLIN, AMERICAN SINGER

25. This is Catwoman's "real" name.

☐ **a.** Emma Frost
☐ **b.** Jean Gray
☐ **c.** Kate Kane
☐ **d.** Selina Kyle

26. Cleopatra was actually of this ethnicity.

☐ **a.** Egyptian
☐ **b.** Italian
☐ **c.** Greek
☐ **d.** Saudi

27. Roe v. Wade was a landmark decision for women's rights. It occurred in what year?

☐ **a.** 1956
☐ **b.** 1969
☐ **c.** 1973
☐ **d.** 1980

28. Shakespeare's *Othello* and *A Winter's Tale* both had female characters with what name?

☐ **a.** Emilia
☐ **b.** Gretchen
☐ **c.** Shiva
☐ **d.** Bethany

29. The first Mother's Day was organized in 1908, but it didn't become an official day of observance in the United States until this year.

☐ **a.** 1909
☐ **b.** 1914
☐ **c.** 1920
☐ **d.** 1931

30. In 1893, this country became the first to officially give women the right to vote.

☐ **a.** Australia
☐ **b.** France
☐ **c.** New Zealand
☐ **d.** Sweden

Did You Know? During the nineteenth century, most factory workers were young, single women.

31. This novel, penned by a woman, is considered by many to be the first novel ever written.

☐ **a.** *The Tale of Genji*
☐ **b.** *The Blazing World*
☐ **c.** *The Fatal Fondness*
☐ **d.** *Agnes de Castro*

32. This woman was the first professional black tennis player . . . and the first to win Wimbledon and the U.S. Open.

☐ **a.** Venus Williams
☐ **b.** Serena Williams
☐ **c.** Althea Gibson
☐ **d.** Zina Garrison

33. Though hockey is usually considered a man's game, this woman is the only one to ever play in an exhibition game in the NI IL.

☐ **a.** Cammi Granato
☐ **b.** Manon Rheaume
☐ **c.** Christine "Chris" Amaru
☐ **d.** Mary Tyler

Did You Know? Super babe and girl next door Elizabeth Shue graduated from Harvard with a degree in government.

34. Considered a men's-only event prior to 1972, the famous Boston Marathon was run by this woman in that year.

☐ **a.** Sara Mae Berman
☐ **b.** Nina Kuscsik
☐ **c.** Roberta Gibb
☐ **d.** Kathrine Switzer

35. This woman was the first to win the Pulitzer Prize for fiction.

☐ **a.** Edith Wharton
☐ **b.** Penelope Farmer
☐ **c.** Harper Lee
☐ **d.** Margaret Mitchell

36. George Eliot was the pen name of what female author?

☐ **a.** Mary Ann Evans
☐ **b.** Emily Brontë
☐ **c.** Karen Blixen
☐ **d.** Acton Bell

37. This female journalist, pen name Nellie Bly, was so dedicated to her work that she faked a mental disorder to complete an expose on mental health facilities. What was her real name?

☐ **a.** Elizabeth Jane Cochrane
☐ **b.** Eileen Welsome
☐ **c.** Mary Heaton Vorse
☐ **d.** Amy Goodman

38. In 1901, Annie Edson Taylor became the first woman (in fact, the first person) to do what?

☐ **a.** Fly in a blimp
☐ **b.** Cross the United States of America in a train
☐ **c.** Go over Niagara Falls in a barrel
☐ **d.** Bungee jump

39. Which was the first state to technically grant women the right to vote?

☐ **a.** Massachusetts
☐ **b.** Wyoming
☐ **c.** California
☐ **d.** Florida

"In politics if you want anything said, ask a man. If you want anything done, ask a woman."

—MARGARET THATCHER, BRITISH POLITICIAN

40. This woman is the female patron saint of France.

☐ **a.** Saint Agatha
☐ **b.** Saint Joan of Arc
☐ **c.** Saint Rose of Lima
☐ **d.** Saint Barbara

41. Emily Dickinson was a famous what?

☐ **a.** Singer
☐ **b.** Inventor
☐ **c.** Poet
☐ **d.** Painter

42. This female singer is known as "The Queen of Soul."

☐ **a.** Aretha Franklin
☐ **b.** Diana Ross
☐ **c.** Gladys Knight
☐ **d.** Tina Turner

43. This folk singer and Woodstock performer had a longtime relationship with music legend Bob Dylan.

☐ **a.** Janis Joplin
☐ **b.** Grace Slick
☐ **c.** Joan Baez
☐ **d.** Nancy Nevins

44. Florence Nightingale Graham is the founder of what company?

☐ **a.** Chanel
☐ **b.** Mary Kay
☐ **c.** Elizabeth Arden
☐ **d.** Estee Lauder

> **True Story**
> In 1966, Alison Steele—known as "The Night Bird"—went on the air at New York City's radio station WNEW, becoming the first female DJ.

45. Ruth Handler invented the Barbie doll and named it after her daughter. After its release in 1959, her toy company Mattel took how long to become a *Fortune* 500 company?

☐ **a.** Five years
☐ **b.** Eight years
☐ **c.** Ten years
☐ **d.** Fourteen years

46. Tabitha Babbitt invented this super manly tool.

☐ **a.** Hammer
☐ **b.** Phillips head screwdriver
☐ **c.** Pipe wrench
☐ **d.** Circular saw

47. This first lady was about as influential as they come, and earned more than forty-eight honorary degrees in her lifetime. She died in 1968.

☐ **a.** Eleanor Roosevelt
☐ **b.** Bess Truman
☐ **c.** Grace Coolidge
☐ **d.** Jackie Kennedy

48. This woman was the first female prime minister of England.

- ☐ **a.** Susan B. Anthony
- ☐ **b.** Margaret Thatcher
- ☐ **c.** Cynthia Booker
- ☐ **d.** Ida Tarbell

49. Which actress was immortalized forever in boys' minds after playing *Wonder Woman*?

- ☐ **a.** Linda Blair
- ☐ **b.** Lynda Carter
- ☐ **c.** Linda Evans
- ☐ **d.** Linda Thompson

50. Who's Spiderman's special lady?

- ☐ **a.** Mary Jane
- ☐ **b.** Sophie
- ☐ **c.** Lilly
- ☐ **d.** Janie

51. This *Charlie's Angels* star was the biggest of them all, becoming a huge sex symbol in the '70s.

- ☐ **a.** Jaclyn Smith
- ☐ **b.** Farrah Fawcett
- ☐ **c.** Cheryl Ladd
- ☐ **d.** Kate Jackson

52. What color plane does Wonder Woman get around in?

- ☐ **a.** Blue
- ☐ **b.** Red
- ☐ **c.** Red, white, and blue
- ☐ **d.** Unknown

> **Did You Know?** Tomoe Gozen is the most famous of Japan's female samurai, described by historians as both beautiful and deadly. She was cutting heads off right and left in the twelfth century.

53. Jean Grey of the X-Men has what power?

☐ **a.** The power to control and produce fire
☐ **b.** Master of magnetism and metal
☐ **c.** Telekinesis
☐ **d.** Control of the weather

54. Which of these actions is *not* just for women?

☐ **a.** The ability to get pregnant
☐ **b.** The ability to lactate from their nipples
☐ **c.** The ability to have multiple orgasms
☐ **d.** The ability to empathize with a suffering child

55. Which funny lady was not a cast member of *Saturday Night Live*?

☐ **a.** Gilda Radner
☐ **b.** Julia Louis-Dreyfus
☐ **c.** Joan Cusack
☐ **d.** Cheryl Hines

56. Queen Elizabeth II became queen in what year?

☐ **a.** 1933
☐ **b.** 1946
☐ **c.** 1952
☐ **d.** 1968

57. Women (and men, too) love to watch the food show on TV. The cooking show genre pretty much started with this television legend.

☐ **a.** Lucille Ball
☐ **b.** Julia Child
☐ **c.** Martha Stewart
☐ **d.** Oprah

58. Esther Rolle played this loving wife on *Good Times*, opposite John Amos.

☐ **a.** Patricia Walker
☐ **b.** Camilla Page
☐ **c.** Florida Evans
☐ **d.** Jackie Hughes

59. *Leave It to Beaver*'s June Cleaver always wore heels and pearls. The actress who played June stated that the pearls hid the shadows on her neck and the heels helped her to look taller than her TV sons. What was the actress's name?

☐ **a.** Barbara Billingsley
☐ **b.** Jane Fonda
☐ **c.** Marion Cunningham
☐ **d.** Diana Hyland

60. Shirley Jones played the mother on *The Partridge Family*, but was the real-life stepmother of which actor on the show?

☐ **a.** Danny Bonaduce
☐ **b.** Susan Dey
☐ **c.** Suzanne Crough
☐ **d.** David Cassidy

61. This actress famously played Dorothy on *The Golden Girls*.

   ☐ **a.** Betty White
   ☐ **b.** Bea Arthur
   ☐ **c.** Rue McClanahan
   ☐ **d.** Estelle Getty

62. During the 1992 presidential campaign, Dan Quayle cited this TV mom as a poor representation of family values.

   ☐ **a.** Roseanne Conner
   ☐ **b.** Marge Simpson
   ☐ **c.** Murphy Brown
   ☐ **d.** Lucy Ricardo

63. What was Mary Tyler Moore's character's name on *The Mary Tyler Moore Show*?

   ☐ **a.** Mary Tyler Moore
   ☐ **b.** Mary Denton
   ☐ **c.** Mary Richards
   ☐ **d.** Mary Goodwin

64. Which famous female gave us this quote, "If you don't like something, change it. If you can't change it, change your attitude. Don't complain."?

   ☐ **a.** Emily Dickinson
   ☐ **b.** Margaret Thatcher
   ☐ **c.** Maya Angelou
   ☐ **d.** Rosa Parks

65. This African-American woman helped to free slaves using the underground railroad.

   ☐ **a.** Josephine Baker
   ☐ **b.** Harriet Tubman

☐ **c.** Margaret Garner
☐ **d.** Sojourner Truth

Did You Know? Jodie Foster graduated as valedictorian from prep school and magna cum laude from Yale.

66. According to the U.S. Census, what percentage of women over eighteen voted in the 2004 presidential elections (compared to 62 percent of men)?

☐ **a.** 37 percent
☐ **b.** 48 percent
☐ **c.** 59 percent
☐ **d.** 65 percent

67. According to the U.S. Census, in 2007 what percent of U.S. armed service members were women?

☐ **a.** 3 percent
☐ **b.** 9 percent
☐ **c.** 14 percent
☐ **d.** 21 percent

68. Bread winners have traditionally been men, but 2007 data suggests that what percent of women make at least $5,000 more than their husbands?

☐ **a.** 9 percent
☐ **b.** 18 percent
☐ **c.** 27 percent
☐ **d.** 36 percent

69. Fact or Fiction: More than half of the people in America over 85 are women.

☐ **a.** Fact
☐ **b.** Fiction

70. According to the 1976 U.S. Census, of women aged 40–44, 90 percent were likely to be mothers. What was that percentage in 2008?

☐ **a.** 53 percent
☐ **b.** 71 percent
☐ **c.** 82 percent
☐ **d.** 94 percent

71. Which sex (aged 25–29) is more likely to hold a bachelor's degree?

☐ **a.** Men
☐ **b.** Women

72. Mary I gained what nickname for her rule of the land?

☐ **a.** Fair Mary
☐ **b.** Mary the Just
☐ **c.** Bloody Mary
☐ **d.** Mary Lamb

73. Countess Elizabeth Bathory, known as the "Blood Countess," murdered at least eighty people in the early 1600s. How was she punished for her crime?

☐ **a.** Burned at the stake
☐ **b.** Walled up in a castle
☐ **c.** Dragged by a horse
☐ **d.** Stoned to death

> **True Story**
> In 1977, Janet Guthrie became the first woman to race in the Indianapolis 500.

74. The pastry known as a Victoria (two pieces of sponge cake with jam in the middle) was named after this woman.

☐ **a.** Victoria Wolff
☐ **b.** Queen Victoria
☐ **c.** Victoria Principal
☐ **d.** Victoria Beckham

75. This creepy female character refused to take off her wedding dress in *Great Expectations.*

☐ **a.** Miss Goldstein
☐ **b.** Miss Havisham
☐ **c.** Miss Moody
☐ **d.** Miss Wilson

76. Madame Bovary is certainly a well-known fictional character, but can you tell us her first name (Hint: it's not Madame.)?

☐ **a.** Jane
☐ **b.** Gertrude
☐ **c.** Emma
☐ **d.** Elizabeth

77. Neil Sedaka's "Oh, Carol" was written about his musician girlfriend, who was:

☐ **a.** Carole Douglass
☐ **b.** Carole King
☐ **c.** Carole Vaughn
☐ **d.** Carol Klein

78. The Beatles' song "Dear Prudence" was about the sister of what famous woman?

☐ **a.** Mia Farrow
☐ **b.** Yoko Ono
☐ **c.** Liz Taylor
☐ **d.** Maya Angelou

79. The CSNY song "Judy Blue Eyes" was written about this woman who was in a relationship with Stephen Stills at the time.

☐ **a.** Judy Dench
☐ **b.** Judy Watson
☐ **c.** Judy Collins
☐ **d.** Judy Jett

80. If you were to go on a first date, which of these topics would be something to stay away from?

☐ **a.** Politics
☐ **b.** Her, in general
☐ **c.** Your dreams or aspirations
☐ **d.** Sex

Did You Know? Sharon Stone flunked out of high school, being all-rebellious as a teen. But it's been reported that she has an IQ of 154.

81. Actress hottie and avid Kentucky Wildcats fan Ashley Judd married an athlete from what sport in the late '90s?

☐ **a.** Auto racing
☐ **b.** Basketball
☐ **c.** Hockey
☐ **d.** Figure skating

82. Actress and midnight fantasy Bridgette Wilson (of *Happy Gilmore* fame) married what famous athlete in 1999?

☐ **a.** Pete Sampras
☐ **b.** Michael Jordan
☐ **c.** Wayne Gretzky
☐ **d.** Pedro Martinez

83. Women used this to redden their lips during the period of Louis the XIV. And they still can, if they're low on lipstick!

☐ **a.** Rose petals
☐ **b.** Cherries
☐ **c.** Milk
☐ **d.** Lemons

84. This was the first cigarette company to market a red filter in order to mask lipstick marks.

☐ **a.** Camel
☐ **b.** Virginia Slims
☐ **c.** Marlboro
☐ **d.** Winston

85. The famous song "In Your Eyes" by Peter Gabriel was written for then-girlfriend Patricia Arquette, and was famously used in what movie?

☐ **a.** *The Breakfast Club*
☐ **b.** *Say Anything*
☐ **c.** *Pretty in Pink*
☐ **d.** *True Romance*

86. Name the chick flick: Zellweger, Cruise, football.

☐ **a.** *All the Right Moves*
☐ **b.** *Bridges of Madison County*
☐ **c.** *Jerry Maguire*
☐ **d.** *Bridget Jones' Diary*

87. Name the chick flick: Neve Campbell, Fairuza Balk, witches.

☐ **a.** *The Craft*
☐ **b.** *Witches of Eastwick*
☐ **c.** *Hocus Pocus*
☐ **d.** *Bedazzled*

88. This woman was the first to shoot down an enemy fighter during WWII.

☐ **a.** Valeria Khomyakova
☐ **b.** Suzanne Powers
☐ **c.** Hillary Newton
☐ **d.** Petrina Gustov

89. Which actress received the first lifetime achievement award from the American Film Institute?

☐ **a.** Marilyn Monroe
☐ **b.** Bette Davis
☐ **c.** Scarlett O'Hara
☐ **d.** Liz Taylor

90. This wild west gunslinger was known as the "Little Sure Shot of the West."

☐ **a.** Calamity Jane
☐ **b.** Belle Star
☐ **c.** Annie Oakley
☐ **d.** Charlie Parkhurst

91. If the girl you're after likes art, or something similar, your best course of action is to just take her to a gallery/lecture and fake it.

☐ **a.** Yes
☐ **b.** No

Did You Know? Ever hear of Boudicca? She was the badass queen of the British Ineni tribe who led an uprising against occupying Roman forces—destroying three cities in the process. Her name means, no joke, Victory.

---

92. The average height of a woman in the United States is roughly:

☐ **a.** 4'11"
☐ **b.** 5'1"
☐ **c.** 5'4"
☐ **d.** 5'6"

93. Ella Fitzgerald won twelve Grammy awards for her work, and also received this national award from the U.S. government.

☐ **a.** Medal of Honor
☐ **b.** Volunteer Service Award
☐ **c.** Medal of Freedom
☐ **d.** Medal of Greatness

94. She was the first female supreme court justice.

☐ **a.** Sandra Day O'Connor
☐ **b.** Sonia Sotomayor
☐ **c.** Elena Kagan
☐ **d.** Ruth Bader Ginsburg

95. Why do women's shirts have buttons on the right side instead of the left side, the way men's shirts do?

☐ **a.** Because women used to be dressed by servants and it was easier that way
☐ **b.** Because more women are left-handed than right-handed
☐ **c.** Because it makes it easier for men to get women's shirts off
☐ **d.** None of the above

96. Oprah Winfrey has an Academy Award to her credit for which of these films?

☐ **a.** *The Color Purple*
☐ **b.** *Beloved*
☐ **c.** *Native Son*
☐ **d.** None of the above

97. Which of these actresses has *not* won both a Best Actress Oscar and a Best Supporting Actress Oscar?

☐ **a.** Meryl Streep
☐ **b.** Jessica Lange
☐ **c.** Sally Field
☐ **d.** Ingrid Bergman

Classic Quote
"Find out who you are and do it on purpose."

—DOLLY PARTON

98. *Terms of Endearment* had two women nominated for Best Actress at the Academy Awards: Shirley MacLaine and Deborah Winger. Which actress took home the award?

☐ **a.** Debra Winger
☐ **b.** Shirley MacLaine
☐ **c.** Neither
☐ **d.** Both

99. 1977's *The Turning Point* also sent two women to the Academy Awards as Best Actress: Anne Bancroft and, again, Shirley MacLaine. Who took home the trophy?

☐ **a.** Anne Bancroft
☐ **b.** Shirley MacLaine
☐ **c.** Neither
☐ **d.** Both

100. What female comedian gave us this quote? "Women complain about premenstrual syndrome, but I think of it as the only time of the month that I can be myself."

☐ **a.** Lucille Ball
☐ **b.** Roseanne Barr
☐ **c.** Whoopi Goldberg
☐ **d.** Lily Tomlin

ANSWER KEY
CHAPTER 8. GENDER RELATIONS: IMPRESSING THE LADIES

1. b.

2. b. She did it in 1903.

3. c.

4. c.

5. b.

6. a. It is the only cell that can be seen with the naked eye.

7. a.

8. b.

9. b. In 1872, Victoria Woodhull became the first woman to run for president. While woman were not allowed to vote, there was no law against a woman becoming president.

10. a.

11. b. They've been on like every car since 1903 . . . so we're guessing she was pretty happy with that patent.

12. c. She also discovered polonium.

13. a. According to the poll, 70 percent of men shower daily while only 57 percent of women do the same. And they say *we're* pigs!

14. b.

15. d.

16. c.

17. a. It was the only gold medal the United States took home that year.

18. i. c; ii. e; iii. b; iv. a; v. d

19. c.

20. a.

21. c.

22. a.

23. b. It's unlikely, but certainly not impossible.

24. a. After Dr. Ernst Grafenberg, the man who discovered it. Sounds like he did some tough scientific research for that one.

25. d.

26. c. Not Egyptian, as many believe.

27. c.

28. a.

29. b.

30. c.

31. a.

32. c. She won each of those tournaments twice, by the way.

33. b.

34. c. Known as "Bobbi" Gibb, she ran the race in 1968 wearing a hoodie in order to hide her identity as a woman.

35. a. In 1921 for *The Age of Innocence*.

36. a.

37. a.

38. c.

39. b.

40. b. For her heroics and her martyrdom at age nineteen.

41. c. Her poems were in fact published posthumously.

42. a. No explanation needed.

43. c.

44. c. She was also big on the horse racing scene, owning many herself.

45. a. Mattel is the combined names of Ruth's husband Elliot and his business partner Matt.

46. d. Carpenters everywhere rejoiced.

47. a.

48. b.

49. b.

50. a.

51. b.

52. d. It's invisible.

53. c.

54. b. With the help of hormones, any man can lactate.

55. d. Her on-screen husband Larry David was a writer for the show, however.

56. c.

57. b. She introduced the United States to French cuisine, starting with *The French Chef* in 1963.

58. c.

59. a.

60. d. Jones married David's father Jack when David was six years old.

61. b.

62. c. Apparently raising a child on your own as a single mother is bad for family values.

63. c.

64. c.

65. b. If you didn't get this, please revisit the second grade.

66. d. Looks like they are exercising their rights just fine.

67. c. Consider that in 1950, that number was 2 percent.

68. b.

69. a.

70. c.

71. b. The U.S. Census for 2007 shows that 33 percent of women in that age group have bachelor's degrees compared with 26 percent of men.

72. c.

73. b.

74. b. It was named after Queen Victoria, who was a fan of the treat.

75. b.

76. c.

77. b.

78. a.

79. c. The song lives on forever, but the couple was doomed.

80. a.

81. a.

82. a.

83. d.

84. c.

85. b. Who could forget John Cusack and that huge boom box?

86. c.

87. a. Hot witches in skirts, hopefully no warts.

88. a.

89. b.

90. c.

91. b.

92. c.

93. c. The highest award given to civilians; other recipients include Maya Angelou and Lucille Ball.

94. a. Appointed by President Reagan in 1981.

95. a.

96. d. Although she was nominated for a Best Supporting Actress award for her role in *The Color Purple*.

97. c. She does have two Best Actress statues, however.

98. b.

99. c. They both lost to Diane Keaton for *Annie Hall*.

100. b.

SCORE!

81–100: Staring at you is a little like watching Wonder Woman make out with Joan of Arc.

61–80: Not bad. You're pretty knowledgeable when it comes to the ladies. Now go put that skill to use and get yourself a female.

41–60: You probably should've taken that women's studies class . . . .

21–40: You're like Queen Amidala—just ruining things left and right.

0–20: Oh God, you remind us of a wrinkled old homeless stripper. Be gone.

CHAPTER 9

MISCELLANY: STUFF YOU SHOULD JUST KNOW, DAMMIT

All right, you're almost at the end. We've tested your testicular aptitude on a number of different topics. But now it's time for the other stuff—the miscellany—the little things that a guy should know, but that don't fit neatly into a specific category. In many ways, this right here is the important stuff. So don't fail us now.

1. Painting rooms on your own saves a ton of money, not just on the paint itself, but on all those damn painters. But you have to know what you're doing. So, if you buy a gallon of paint, how big of an area will you be able to paint?

   ☐ **a.** 100 sq. ft.
   ☐ **b.** 400 sq. ft.
   ☐ **c.** 800 sq. ft.
   ☐ **d.** 1,200 sq. ft.

2. This knot is preferred by rock climbers as a stopper for two main reasons: It's easily tied, and it retains more than ¾ of the rope's strength.

   ☐ **a.** Double bowline
   ☐ **b.** Figure 8
   ☐ **c.** Rolling hitch
   ☐ **d.** Butterfly knot

3. Which of the following is *not* a type of household hammer?

   ☐ **a.** Claw hammer
   ☐ **b.** Ball-peen hammer
   ☐ **c.** Gun hammer
   ☐ **d.** Sledge hammer

4. The crescent wrench is one of the handiest tools to have around the house. But you might know it by its other name.

   ☐ **a.** Adjustable wrench
   ☐ **b.** Fork wrench
   ☐ **c.** Butt wrench
   ☐ **d.** Crank wrench

> **True Story**
> Iran is the only country in the world where you can sell your kidney for cash.

5. We all want to keep our streets clean of drugs, but what's the cost? How much has the United States spent in the last forty years on the "War on Drugs"?

☐ **a.** $1 billion
☐ **b.** $35 billion
☐ **c.** $500 billion
☐ **d.** $1 trillion

6. Fact or Fiction: The Grand Canyon is the #1 tourist destination in the United States.

☐ **a.** Fact
☐ **b.** Fiction

7. Fact or Fiction: Stephen King's *The Dark Tower* series features a magic-wielding cowboy as the protagonist.

☐ **a.** Fact
☐ **b.** Fiction

8. Which of the following was *not* a member of the original class inducted into the Toy Hall of Fame in 1998? (Yes, there is a Toy Hall of Fame, and yes, that's awesome.)

☐ **a.** Play-Doh
☐ **b.** Legos
☐ **c.** Erector Set
☐ **d.** Atari 2600 game system

9. The original G.I. Joe hit the shelves in what year?

☐ **a.** 1953
☐ **b.** 1964
☐ **c.** 1970
☐ **d.** 1981

10. As far as cool jobs go, professional gamer, a.k.a. playing video games for money, ranks pretty high on the list. According to the *Guinness Book of World Records*, the youngest pro gamer ever turned pro at what age?

☐ **a.** Four
☐ **b.** Seven
☐ **c.** Fifteen
☐ **d.** Eleven

11. Up, Up, Down, Down, Left, Right, Left, Right, B, A, Start. This code should make you think of what?

☐ **a.** Contra
☐ **b.** Galaga
☐ **c.** Pac-Man
☐ **d.** Mario Bros.

12. Mario of Super Mario Bros. fame is actually a spin-off from what other Nintendo game?

☐ **a.** Zelda
☐ **b.** Duck Hunt
☐ **c.** Donkey Kong
☐ **d.** Double Dragon

13. Which of these men has *not* appeared on the cover of *Playboy*?

☐ **a.** Jerry Seinfeld
☐ **b.** Burt Reynolds
☐ **c.** Steve Martin
☐ **d.** Sean Connery

14. Everyone knows *Playboy*, but do you know what the original name for the magazine was?

☐ **a.** *Swingers*
☐ **b.** *Stag Party*
☐ **c.** *Class Act*
☐ **d.** *For Your Eyes Only*

Classic Quote
"I live for myself and I answer to nobody."
—STEVE MCQUEEN

15. For less irritation while shaving, you should:

☐ **a.** Go against the grain
☐ **b.** Go with the grain

Classic Quote
"Violent men have not been known in history to die to a man. They die up to a point."
—MAHATMA GANDHI

16. Fact or Fiction: Women know when we're lying.

☐ **a.** Fact
☐ **b.** Fiction

17. Fact or Fiction: If you need to cross a cold river, the best thing to do is keep your clothes on to help insulate your body from the cold water.

☐ **a.** Fact
☐ **b.** Fiction

18. Guys aren't allergic to laundry, but let's just say we tend to do it less than we should. In a perfect world, how often should you wash and change your bed sheets?

☐ **a.** Every one to two weeks
☐ **b.** Once a month
☐ **c.** Every three months
☐ **d.** Once every year or two should do it

19. Everyone loves a big-ass widescreen HDTV. But do you know how to properly measure the size of your TV?

☐ **a.** Left to right
☐ **b.** Top to bottom
☐ **c.** Diagonally
☐ **d.** Calculate the area

> **Did You Know?** Something called Baconnaise actually exists—it's a kosher spread that tastes like bacon.

20. If you usually wear a suit to work, what's the general rule of thumb on how many you should own?

☐ **a.** Five
☐ **b.** Six
☐ **c.** Ten
☐ **d.** Twelve

21. What type of fuel is *not* used with blowtorches?

☐ **a.** Butane
☐ **b.** Propane
☐ **c.** Liquid petroleum
☐ **d.** Silane

22. This is a list of the tools that every guy should have if he owns a home. If you have all of them, congratulations, give yourself a point.

☐ Hammer
☐ Screwdrivers (assorted)
☐ Needle nose pliers
☐ Utility knife
☐ Reversible drill
☐ Tape measure
☐ Vise grips
☐ Wire cutter/stripper
☐ ½" steel chisel
☐ Handsaw

23. The workbench isn't the only thing to keep stocked. Check each item below that you have in your medicine cabinet. After all, it's easy to hurt yourself with tools even if you know what you're doing. If you've got them all, throw yourself a point.

☐ Alcohol wipes/Hydrogen Peroxide
☐ Adhesive bandages, assorted sizes (you know, Band-Aids)
☐ Thermometer
☐ Pain reliever (Tylenol, Advil)
☐ Antacid
☐ Antihistamine
☐ Decongestant (for those darn colds)
☐ Gauze pads and tape
☐ Tweezers
☐ Cough drops

24. Fact or Fiction: If you are going bald, hide it using a toupee. Nobody will know.

☐ **a.** Fact
☐ **b.** Fiction

25. Which of these failed video game consoles was an offer from the original Atari?

☐ **a.** 3DO
☐ **b.** Saturn
☐ **c.** Jaguar
☐ **d.** Dreamcast

26. In Australia, the noncoin currency is made of what material?

☐ **a.** Paper
☐ **b.** Metal
☐ **c.** Plastic
☐ **d.** Hemp

27. Sometimes snakes are born with two heads. What happens if one head smells food on the other head?

☐ **a.** It tries to move away from the smell
☐ **b.** It tries to eat the second head
☐ **c.** It forces the other head to feed it
☐ **d.** It does nothing; both heads share a body and thus a digestive system.

28. This was the first product to have a barcode on it.

☐ **a.** Wrigley's gum
☐ **b.** Coca-Cola
☐ **c.** Skippy peanut butter
☐ **d.** Cheerios

29. Fact or Fiction: Of all the muscles in the body, the tongue is the only one that is attached at one end and not the other.

☐ **a.** Fact
☐ **b.** Fiction

Top 5 List

Five Books Every Guy Should Read

1984
Catch-22
For Whom the Bell Tolls
Catcher in the Rye
Lord of the Flies

---

30. The name Portland, Oregon, was chosen on the flip of a coin by its two founders, both of whom wanted to name the city after their hometown. What was the alternate choice for the city?

☐ **a.** Boston
☐ **b.** Buffalo
☐ **c.** Reading
☐ **d.** Springfield

31. Fact or Fiction: The word "golf" originally stood for "Gentleman Only, Ladies Forbidden."

☐ **a.** Fact
☐ **b.** Fiction

32. Fact or Fiction: All planets are named after gods.

☐ **a.** Fact
☐ **b.** Fiction

33. To remove blood from clothing, you should use:

    ☐ **a.** Hot water
    ☐ **b.** Cold water
    ☐ **c.** Tepid water
    ☐ **d.** Club soda

34. What band was Jimmy Page in before Led Zeppelin?

    ☐ **a.** The Electrics
    ☐ **b.** The Yardbirds
    ☐ **c.** Bad Company
    ☐ **d.** Pink Floyd

35. Which of these musicians was *not* a member of the Travelling Wilburys?

    ☐ **a.** Tom Petty
    ☐ **b.** Bob Dylan
    ☐ **c.** Rick Danko
    ☐ **d.** George Harrison

36. Doctors recommend that you get your prostate examined (we know, we know it's not a ton of fun) every year starting at this age:

    ☐ **a.** Twenty-five
    ☐ **b.** Thirty
    ☐ **c.** Forty
    ☐ **d.** Fifty

Classic Quote
"Nearly all men can stand adversity, but if you want to test a man's character, give him power."
—ABRAHAM LINCOLN

37. Fact or Fiction: Smoking can make your penis shrink.

☐ **a.** Fact
☐ **b.** Fiction

38. The average male orgasm lasts six seconds. How long do female orgasms last, on average?

☐ **a.** 23 seconds
☐ **b.** 44 seconds
☐ **c.** 58 seconds
☐ **d.** 121 seconds

39. Is there any way for an American to buy a Cuban cigar legally?

☐ **a.** Yes
☐ **b.** No

40. The practice of closing a wound with Krazy Glue started where?

☐ **a.** The Vietnam War
☐ **b.** The ER
☐ **c.** The NFL
☐ **d.** NASA Missions

41. How should you react when confronted by a bear?

☐ **a.** Run as fast as you can toward the bear
☐ **b.** Crap your pants
☐ **c.** Stand tall, even if the bear charges you
☐ **d.** Climb the nearest tree

42. To get out of a rip current, what should you do?

☐ **a.** Swim toward the beach
☐ **b.** Follow the shoreline sideways
☐ **c.** Swim away from the beach
☐ **d.** Dive to get under the current

True Story
Weed smokers have a lower risk of obesity. Put that in your pipe and smoke it!

43. The Marlboro Man died of what?

☐ **a.** Lung cancer
☐ **b.** Suicide
☐ **c.** Motorcycle accident
☐ **d.** Drowning

44. The "Death's Head" logo is worn by the proud members of this infamous motorcycle club.

☐ **a.** The Mongols
☐ **b.** The Hell's Angels
☐ **c.** The Outlaws
☐ **d.** The Highwaymen

45. How tall is the average American man?

☐ **a.** Between 5'9" and 5'10"
☐ **b.** Between 5'11" and 6'
☐ **c.** Between 6' and 6'1"
☐ **d.** Between 6'1" and 6'2"

Classic Quote

"Cock your hat—angles are attitudes."

—FRANK SINATRA

46. Which of the following was *not* a member of the rap group NWA?

☐ **a.** Eazy-E
☐ **b.** Ice Cube
☐ **c.** Dr. Dre
☐ **d.** The D.O.C.

47. Which one of these is *not* a Notorious B.I.G. song?

☐ **a.** "Going back to Cali"
☐ **b.** "Juicy"
☐ **c.** "Lodi Dodi"
☐ **d.** "Hypnotize"

48. Tupac's *Greatest Hits* album featured a previously unreleased song that samples "The Way It Is" by Bruce Hornsby and the Range. Name that song.

☐ **a.** "How Do You Want It"
☐ **b.** "Changes"
☐ **c.** "Dear Mama"
☐ **d.** "Unconditional Love"

49. In blackjack, you always split:

☐ **a.** Kings
☐ **b.** Eights or aces
☐ **c.** Jacks or queens
☐ **d.** 7s

50. In blackjack, you always double-down on:

☐ **a.** Sixteen
☐ **b.** Nine
☐ **c.** Eleven
☐ **d.** Thirteen

51. What is a light-year?

☐ **a.** The measure of distance that light travels over 365.25 days
☐ **b.** The amount of light that passes back and forth between the Earth and Moon in a year
☐ **c.** The amount of time it takes for light to travel to the Sun and back
☐ **d.** A year that's not too heavy

52. Why does sweat smell?

☐ **a.** Feeding bacteria
☐ **b.** Dying cells
☐ **c.** Too much moisture
☐ **d.** No deodorant

53. Known as the "dead man's hand," this is what Wild Bill Hickok was holding when Jack McCall shot him dead during a poker game.

☐ **a.** Nine-high flush
☐ **b.** Pair of eights and a pair of aces
☐ **c.** Three sevens
☐ **d.** Full house, fives full of sixes

> **True Story**
> All the human urine produced worldwide in a single day would take just twenty minutes to flow over Niagara Falls.

54. What is the best bait to catch a mouse?

☐ **a.** Cheese
☐ **b.** Peanut butter
☐ **c.** Chocolate
☐ **d.** Hammer

55. If no artificial coloring were added, what color would Coca-Cola be?

☐ **a.** Green
☐ **b.** Blue
☐ **c.** Brown
☐ **d.** Purple

56. You can catch a cold by doing any of the following except:

☐ **a.** Not washing your hands
☐ **b.** Being outside when it's chilly
☐ **c.** Being around someone who is sick
☐ **d.** Using someone else's silverware

57. In the classic board game Risk, what country does Brazil attach to that is not located in South America?

☐ **a.** South Africa
☐ **b.** North Africa
☐ **c.** India
☐ **d.** Southern Europe

58. Which of these wonders can be seen from space?

☐ **a.** The Great Wall of China
☐ **b.** The Pyramids
☐ **c.** The Trans-Siberian Railway
☐ **d.** A and C

Top 5 List

Five Things You Should Do Before You Die (that are actually achievable)	Visit Amsterdam's Red Light district
	Drive on the Autobahn
	Hit a home run, even if it's just in softball
	See the Grand Canyon
	Go parachuting

---

59. What is the best way of killing someone with your bare hands?

☐ **a.** Crush their windpipe
☐ **b.** Gouge their eyes
☐ **c.** Nosebone through the brain
☐ **d.** Pull them apart by the legs

60. Who is the hardest-working man in show business?

☐ **a.** David Letterman
☐ **b.** James Brown
☐ **c.** Eddie Murphy
☐ **d.** Tom Cruise's publicist

> **Did You Know?** The X-Men debuted in *X-Men #1* in 1963.

61. Men can sometimes go how long without farting?

☐ **a.** Two days
☐ **b.** Four days
☐ **c.** One week
☐ **d.** None of the above

62. What color is St. James Place in Monopoly?

☐ **a.** Green
☐ **b.** Red
☐ **c.** Orange
☐ **d.** Purple

63. Which of these is *not* a Jack London book?

☐ **a.** *The Game*
☐ **b.** *The Human Drift*
☐ **c.** *The Valley of the Moon*
☐ **d.** *Goose in Winter*

> **Did You Know?** Superman made his debut in *Action Comics #1* in 1938.

64. Who wrote *Brave New World*?

☐ **a.** Aldous Huxley
☐ **b.** Sir Arthur Conan Doyle
☐ **c.** John Milton
☐ **d.** H.G. Wells

65. According to Robert Greene, how many Laws of Power exist?

☐ **a.** 48
☐ **b.** 73
☐ **c.** 141
☐ **d.** 190

66. Grand Theft Auto III and IV are set in this fictional city.

☐ **a.** Vice City
☐ **b.** San Andreas
☐ **c.** San Vegas
☐ **d.** Liberty City

67. In Super Mario Kart, red shells are known for doing what?

☐ **a.** Having ricochet abilities
☐ **b.** Being heat seeking
☐ **c.** Being giant
☐ **d.** Making you fly

68. Put these video games in order of release

☐ **i.** Donkey Kong   **a.** 1978
☐ **ii.** Space Invaders   **b.** 1979
☐ **iii.** Pac-Man   **c.** 1980
☐ **iv.** Asteroids   **d.** 1981

69. Who is considered the father of jazz?

☐ **a.** Max Roach
☐ **b.** Louis Armstrong
☐ **c.** Miles Davis
☐ **d.** Art Tatum

Classic Quote
"Do not pray for easy lives. Pray to be stronger men."
—JOHN F. KENNEDY

70. It's important to keep a decently stocked man kitchen. Go take a look. If you have all of these in the fridge, give yourself a point.

- ☐ Beer
- ☐ Pretzels
- ☐ Milk
- ☐ Red meat
- ☐ Whiskey
- ☐ Wine (for the ladies)
- ☐ Peanut butter
- ☐ Hot dogs
- ☐ Leftover Chinese food
- ☐ Leftover pizza

71. This snake, considered one of the deadliest snakes on Earth, is named for its mouth and not its scales, as some believe.

- ☐ **a.** Copperhead
- ☐ **b.** Black mamba
- ☐ **c.** Tiger snake
- ☐ **d.** Eastern diamondback

72. The Amazon's Satere-Mawé tribe has a ritual when boys become men that involves filling gloves with this item, then wearing the gloves twenty times for ten minutes; then one is considered a man.

- ☐ **a.** Thorns
- ☐ **b.** Bullet ants
- ☐ **c.** Wasps
- ☐ **d.** Piranha teeth

73. Which of these animals is least likely to carry and transmit rabies to humans?

☐ **a.** Woodchuck
☐ **b.** Wolf
☐ **c.** Bear
☐ **d.** Squirrel

74. Which of these is on the short list of venomous mammals?

☐ **a.** Porcupine
☐ **b.** Hairy-nosed wombat
☐ **c.** Platypus
☐ **d.** Australian mouse

75. Which species of bear does not hibernate?

☐ **a.** Black bear
☐ **b.** Polar bear
☐ **c.** Grizzly bear
☐ **d.** Panda bear

76. Proportionally speaking, this creature has the largest penis to body ratio. (No, it's not you . . .)

☐ **a.** Barnacle
☐ **b.** Flea
☐ **c.** Elephant
☐ **d.** Whale shark

77. This animal can last longer than any other without water.

☐ **a.** Rhino
☐ **b.** Camel
☐ **c.** Kangaroo Rat
☐ **d.** Giraffe

78. What rare event happened when Mark Twain was born *and* when he died?

☐ **a.** Solar eclipse
☐ **b.** Halley's comet
☐ **c.** Lunar eclipse
☐ **d.** Asteroid hitting Earth

79. Julie Nixon, daughter of President Richard Nixon, married what other former president's grandson?

☐ **a.** Dwight D. Eisenhower
☐ **b.** Harry Truman
☐ **c.** Herbert Hoover
☐ **d.** Lyndon B. Johnson

80. This is believed to be St. Patrick's real name.

☐ **a.** Maewyn Succat
☐ **b.** Flann Brogan
☐ **c.** Tanai Egan
☐ **d.** Patrick Devlin

81. A 2 × 4 piece of wood has what dimensions?

☐ **a.** 2 inches by 4 inches
☐ **b.** 1.5 inches by 3.5 inches
☐ **c.** 2.5 inches by 4.5 inches
☐ **d.** 1 inch by 3 inches

82. Fancy yourself a money man, do ya? How many reeds (or ridges) are on a dime?

☐ **a.** 79
☐ **b.** 118
☐ **c.** 191
☐ **d.** 207

83. Every workshop needs a bottle of WD-40. The only question is, what does the WD stand for?

- [ ] **a.** Washing dirt
- [ ] **b.** Wet or dry
- [ ] **c.** Water displacement
- [ ] **d.** Wax dioxide

84. Which planet in our solar system spins opposite of all the others?

- [ ] **a.** Mercury
- [ ] **b.** Earth
- [ ] **c.** Neptune
- [ ] **d.** Venus

85. Like math? Try this one out. How many years are equal to 1 billion seconds?

- [ ] **a.** Nine years
- [ ] **b.** Thirteen years
- [ ] **c.** Twenty-six years
- [ ] **d.** Thirty-two years

86. Which of these is *not* a Tom Clancy novel?

- [ ] **a.** *Without Remorse*
- [ ] **b.** *Red Rabbit*
- [ ] **c.** *The Sum of All Fears*
- [ ] **d.** *The Russia House*

87. Which of these artists did *not* perform at Woodstock?

- [ ] **a.** Joe Cocker
- [ ] **b.** The Band
- [ ] **c.** Bob Dylan
- [ ] **d.** The Who

88. What is the highest possible credit score?

- ☐ **a.** 420
- ☐ **b.** 750
- ☐ **c.** 850
- ☐ **d.** 1,000

89. What's the best way to fight off a shark attack?

- ☐ **a.** Play dead
- ☐ **b.** Attack the shark's snout, gills, and eyes
- ☐ **c.** Grab the nearest fin, and twist
- ☐ **d.** Try to pry the animal's jaw open, causing pain until it turns and swims away

90. Finish this piece of weather lore: *Red sky at night, sailor's delight; Red sky at morning*:

- ☐ **a.** sailor in mourning
- ☐ **b.** sailors take warning
- ☐ **c.** fish will be swarming
- ☐ **d.** waves transforming

91. Which of these men was *not* an Eagle Scout?

- ☐ **a.** Steven Spielberg
- ☐ **b.** Neil Armstrong
- ☐ **c.** Gerald. R. Ford
- ☐ **d.** John F. Kennedy

92. Which of these would be the most effective zombie-killing weapon?

- ☐ **a.** Flamethrower
- ☐ **b.** Grenade
- ☐ **c.** Baseball bat
- ☐ **d.** Shotgun

93. While trying to set the record for world's heaviest hangglider, André the Giant hit the ground so hard that he lost his:

☐ **a.** Sense of smell
☐ **b.** Memory
☐ **c.** Shoes
☐ **d.** Hearing

94. Which of these is *not* a G.I. Joe character?

☐ **a.** Snow Job
☐ **b.** Flash Bang
☐ **c.** Frostbite
☐ **d.** Snake Eyes

95. What's the name of Captain America's alter ego?

☐ **a.** Reed Richards
☐ **b.** Al DeStefano
☐ **c.** Bruce Banner
☐ **d.** Steve Rogers

96. This is the name of the legendary Boston P.I. created by Robert B. Parker.

☐ **a.** Spenser
☐ **b.** Hunter
☐ **c.** Porter
☐ **d.** Reacher

97. Which of these was *not* one of Frank Sinatra's nicknames?

☐ **a.** Ol' Blue Eyes
☐ **b.** Killer
☐ **c.** The Voice
☐ **d.** Chairman of the Board

98. Who created the Conan the Barbarian character?

☐ **a.** Edgar Rice Burroughs
☐ **b.** Barry Windsor-Smith
☐ **c.** Robert E. Howard
☐ **d.** William Faulkner

99. This country music legend is known by the nickname Bocephus.

☐ **a.** Waylon Jennings
☐ **b.** Hank Williams, Jr.
☐ **c.** David Allen Coe
☐ **d.** Merle Haggard

100. In what year was the first Zippo lighter manufactured?

☐ **a.** 1887
☐ **b.** 1914
☐ **c.** 1933
☐ **d.** 1941

ANSWER KEY
CHAPTER 9. MISCELLANY: STUFF YOU SHOULD JUST KNOW, DAMMIT

1. b.

2. b.

3. c.

4. a.

5. d.

6. b. It's actually #20. Times Square is #1.

7. a.

8. d. Though not a member of the inaugural class, the oversight was reversed when it was put in the hall in 2009.

9. b. And Christmas was never the same.

10. b. Victor De Leon III signed a contract at age seven to play games professionally. Try to contain your jealousy.

11. a. D'oh!

12. c.

13. d.

14. b. The name only lasted one issue due to copyright problems.

15. b. Help avoid razor burn.

16. a. You're not as smart as you think you are.

17. b.

18. a.

19. c. From the top corner to the opposite bottom corner, or vice versa, will do the trick.

20. b. One for every work day plus one as a spare or for the weekend.

21. d.

22. 1 point if all are checked.

23. 1 point if all are checked.

24. b.

25. c.

26. c. It's recyclable and harder to counterfeit. Pretty cool.

27. b. Now this we gotta see.

28. a. In 1973 at Marsh's supermarket in Troy, Ohio.

29. a.

30. a. The two conducting the coin flip wanted it named after their respective home towns. Portland got its name from Portland, Maine.

31. b.

32. b. Earth is in fact the only planet not named after a god.

33. b.

34. b.

35. c.

36. c.

37. b.

38. a.

39. a. Only if it is made from pre-embargo tobacco. The only way for an American to legally enjoy this product is to smoke a cigar made with tobacco that left Cuba before the embargo. Hope you have some cash, though; these puppies are expensive.

40. a.

41. c.

42. b.

43. a.

44. b.

45. a.

46. d.

47. c.

48. b.

49. b.

50. c.

51. a.

52. a.

53. b.

54. b. Smells stronger than cheese, and it's sticky, which keeps the mouse on the trap.

55. a.

56. b.

57. b.

58. d.

59. a.

60. b. That's what they called him, but Tom's publicist is moving up the list.

61. d. What, are you nuts!? On average, you'll fart fourteen times a day as part of your natural digestion.

62. c.

63. d.

64. a.

65. a.

66. d.

67. b.

68. i. d; ii. a; iii. c; iv. b

69. b.

70. 1 point if all are checked.

71. b. So-called due to the inky black inside of their mouth, something you really don't want to see.

72. b. While that may sound better than the other options, each sting from these ants is about thirty times more painful than a wasp sting. Ouch!

73. d. While they *can* carry the disease, they are almost never known to have it and are not a cause of rabies in the United States.

74. c. Only males though.

75. d.

76. a.

77. c. They can last their entire life (3–5 years) without water.

78. b.

79. a.

80. a.

81. b. When cut it is 2 × 4 inches, but after the drying process each dimension is reduced by a half inch.

82. b.

83. c.

84. d.

85. d.

86. d.

87. c.

88. c.

89. b.

90. b.

91. d.

92. b.

93. d.

94. a.

95. d.

96. a.

97. b.

98. c.

99. b.

100. c.

SCORE!

81–100: You're like an antique Rolex—awesome in every way.

61–80: You're like a Swiss army knife—from time to time, you come in handy.

41–60: Hey there, Harry Potter. Some people like you, sure. But we're not particularly impressed.

21–40: Go rent *Sling Blade*. Remind you of anyone?

0–20: Worst. Guy. Ever.

THE FINAL SCORE

Well, lookie here. You made it all the way to the end of the book. That feat alone makes you a man in our book. Well, not *this* book—another book we have—where we keep track of stuff. Like grocery lists, etc.

Anyway, time to see how you did overall:

0–100: Are you positive you were holding the book right way? You're supposed to read from left to right . . . you know that, right?

101–200: Do you have two testicles? Are you sure? Why don't you take a minute to count them. Don't worry, we'll wait.

201–300: You need to go on Netflix or walk down to your local video store and rent every John Wayne movie they have. Then watch them back, to back, to back.

301–400: Just slightly below average. You might want to look into getting a collagen injection . . . in your testes.

401–500: Not too shabby. You're about half man. It could certainly be worse.

501–600: Good work. But you've got some studying to do.

601–700: You should let your ball hair grow really, really long, and then have your left nut go as Albert Einstein for Halloween next year. That's the sort of testicular aptitude you possess.

701–800: If they gave out trophies for testicles, you'd have a whole case full. We're very impressed. Now that you've done all this test taking, why don't you go relax by wrestling an alligator or jumping rope with a boa constrictor.

801–900: We'd accuse you of cheating, but we wouldn't want to risk invoking the wrath of your gigantic testicles.

Now if you're satisfied with your score—good! Give yourself a pat on the back. Then take this book and go find a few friends, and see if their testicaular aptitude can stack up next to yours.

If you're not to happy with your score—well, you've got some work to do. Rent some guy movies, do some guy stuff, go shoot some hoops, then come back and take the tests again. That's the beauty of the book—you can always improve!

INDEX

Academy Awards, 14, 31, 234, 252, 253
Adams, Jack, 50
Air Force One, 159
Airplane, 33, 215
Airplanes, 200–10, 214–15, 218, 221–22
Alcohol, 75–84, 86–90, 93, 106–7, 117
ALF, 184
Ali, Muhammad, 53, 54
Allen, Tim, 173
All in the Family, 179
American Gangster, 157
American Graffiti, 208
Amos, John, 243
Anchorman, 27
Anderson, Harry, 175
Anderson, Mary, 232
Animal House, 21, 95
Antoinette, Marie, 81
Apocalypse Now, 18
Army of Darkness, 30
Arquette, Patricia, 249
Artest, Ron, 48
A-Team, 9, 176
Automobiles, 26, 199–227
Auto racing, 45, 118, 202, 206
Aykroyd, Dan, 32, 34

Babbitt, Tabitha, 240
Back to the Future, 26, 206
Bad Boys, 17
Baio, Scott, 176
Balk, Fairuza, 250
Bancroft, Anne, 253
Band of Brothers, 138
Bardeen, John, 155
Barker, Bob, 177
Barkley, Charles, 56
Baseball, 42–52, 55–66, 108, 115, 118,
  128, 188, 276
Basketball, 43–48, 52–60, 63, 111, 117
Bathory, Elizabeth, 246
Battlestar Galactica, 192
Bauer, Jack, 172
Baywatch, 170, 176
BBQs, 74, 85, 86, 87
Beach Boys, 217
Beatles, 117, 209, 248

Beer, 75–80, 84, 88, 90, 107, 117
Bergen, Candice, 188
Beverages, 75–84, 86–90, 93–96, 106–7, 117
Beverly Hills 90210, 191
The Big Lebowski, 20, 33
Bill of Rights, 159
Black Hawk Down, 149
Blazing Saddles, 33
"Blue Angels," 213
Blues Brothers, 25, 26, 211, 220
Bly, Nellie, 238
Board games, 275, 277
Boats, 217, 218
Bogart, Humphrey, 20, 23
Bonanza, 174
Bonaparte, Napoleon, 155, 158
Bond, James, 13, 16, 30, 35, 205
Bonnie and Clyde, 9, 206
Booth, John Wilkes, 155
Boudicca, Queen, 251
Bovary, Madame, 247
Bowling, 56, 60
Boxing, 53–54, 56, 63, 120
Brattain, Walter H., 155
Brave New World, 277
The Bridge on the River Kwai, 23
Bronson, Charles, 11
Brown, Jim, 63
Bryant, Paul, 65
Buckner, Bill, 66
Bullitt, 17
Burr, Aaron, 154

Caddyshack, 15, 31
Caesar, Julius, 141
Campbell, Neve, 250
Candies, 87–89
Candy, John, 220
Cards, playing, 126, 273, 274
Carlson, Dave, 12
Cars, 26, 199–227
Casablanca, 23
Catch-22, 269
Catcher in the Rye, 269
Catch Me If You Can, 150
Catwoman, 235
Chamberlain, Wilt, 111

Charles in Charge, 176
Charlie's Angels, 241
Cheers, 175, 177
Chiklis, Michael, 170
Children, 108, 232
Cigarettes, 189, 249, 271, 272
Cinema, 11–40
Cinema Answer Key, 36–40
Clancy, Tom, 282
Clavin, Cliff, 177
Cleopatra, 235
Cockerell, Christopher, 219
Coffee, 82, 94
Columbus, Christopher, 151
Conan the Barbarian, 27, 34, 285
Condiments, 74, 95, 127
Connery, Sean, 13, 16
Cool Hand Luke, 24
Coppola, Francis Ford, 18
Cruise, Tom, 12, 250
Crumpler, Rebecca Lee, 231
Csonka, Larry, 46
Curb Your Enthusiasm, 171
Curie, Marie, 230, 232

Daimler, Gottlieb, 210
Dallas, 182
Dangerfield, Rodney, 87
The Dark Tower, 263
Dazed and Confused, 18
The Deadliest Catch, 95
Deadwood, 190
The Deer Hunter, 25
Dempsey, Tom, 120
De Niro, Robert, 15, 17, 22, 29, 30
Desperate Housewives, 188
Dickinson, Charles, 151
Dickinson, Emily, 239
Die Hard, 26
Diff'rent Strokes, 173, 192
DiMaggio, Joe, 127
Diner, 20
The Dirty Dozen, 15
Dirty Harry, 9, 13, 14
Ditka, Mike, 58
Donnie Brasco, 13, 143
The Driver, 211

Dr. No, 16
Dukes of Hazzard, 185, 220
Dylan, Bob, 239

Eastwood, Clint, 9, 11, 13, 20, 22, 187, 202
Edison, Thomas, 93
Einstein, Albert, 115
Einstein, Norman, 48
Elam, Jason, 120
Eliot, George, 238
Elizabeth II, Queen, 242
Ellis, Dock, 54
Enola Gay, 151
Enter the Dragon, 23

Family Guy, 172, 178
Family Matters, 177
Fast food, 78–82, 85, 89–92, 96, 130
Females, famous, 229–59
A Few Good Men, 173
Fight Club, 19
Final score, tallying, 203–06
Fitzgerald, Ella, 251
The Flintstones, 179
Food, 73–103, 127, 243, 279
Food Answer Key, 98–103
Football, 44–49, 52–58, 61–65, 107, 120
"For What It's Worth," 146, 147
For Whom the Bell Tolls, 269
Ford, Harrison, 12, 208
Ford, Henry, 93
Foreman, George, 54
Forrest Gump, 146
48 Hrs., 21, 219
Foster, Jodie, 245
The French Connection, 23, 211
The Fresh Prince of Bel-Air, 191
Friends, 174
Full Metal Jacket, 12, 16

Gabriel, Peter, 249
Gandhi, Mahatma, 265
Gender Relations, 229–59
Gender Relations Answer Key, 254–59
Get Shorty, 219
The Ghostbusters, 35

G.I. Joe, 186, 263, 284
"Glory Boys," 160
The Godfather, 170
The Godfather Part II, 15
The Golden Girls, 244
Goldfinger, 30
Golf, 46, 61, 64, 109, 123, 269
Gone in 60 Seconds, 211, 212
The Good, The Bad, and The Ugly, 22
Good Times, 243
Gozen, Tomoe, 242
Graham, Bette Nesmith, 230
Graham, Florence Nightingale, 240
The Great Escape, 19
Great Expectations, 247
Greene, Robert, 277
Grilling, 74, 85, 86, 148
Grylls, Bear, 171
Guinness Book of World Records, 264
Gun Crazy, 32
Guns, 107, 138, 143, 145, 157
Gunsmoke, 178, 179, 184
Guthrie, Janet, 246
"Guy movie," 11–12, 211

Hackman, Gene, 20, 23
Hall of Fame, 70, 107
Hamilton, Alexander, 154
Handler, Ruth, 240
Happy Days, 173, 182
Happy Gilmore, 249
Hard Boiled, 19
Harris, Neil Patrick, 89
Harrison, Craig, 120
Harroun, Ray, 212
Heat, 30
Hercules in New York, 29
Highlander, 30
Hill, Henry, 149
Hillary, Sir Edmund, 114
History, 137–67
History Answer Key, 162–67
Hockey, 43, 45, 47, 50, 62, 237
Hogan, Hulk, 62, 187
Hogan's Heroes, 180
Holiday, Doc, 146
Home Improvement, 173, 177

The Honeymooners, 176, 182
Hornsby, Bruce, 273
Horse racing, 61, 62, 66
Hot dogs, 77, 78, 82, 86
Howell, C. Thomas, 18
Huffman, Felicity, 173
Hughes, John, 220
Hussein, Saddam, 153
The Hustler, 23

In Living Color, 190
The Italian Job, 209

Jackson, Andrew, 151
Jackson, "Shoeless" Joe, 58
Jackson, Stonewall, 145
James, Jesse, 160
Jennings, Ken, 177
Jeopardy!, 177
The Jerk, 34
Jones, Shirley, 243
Joplin, Janis, 216, 235
Jordan, Michael, 117
Judd, Ashley, 248

Kare, Susan, 231
Kennedy, John F., 157, 278
Kidd, Jason, 49
Kilmer, Val, 15, 146
King, Stephen, 263
The King of Queens, 181
Knievel, Evel, 206
Krause, Peter, 173
Kyzer, Dudley Wayne, 124

Langseth, Hans, 129
Larder, Dr. Dionysys, 212
Lassen, Louis, 86
The Last Waltz, 26
Leave It to Beaver, 181, 243
Lee, Bruce, 23
Lennon, John, 175
Leonidas, King, 140
Lethal Weapon, 12
Letterman, David, 188
Lincoln, Abraham, 141, 155, 270
Lindbergh, Charles, 221

Little House on the Prairie, 174
London, Jack, 277
The Longest Yard, 29
Lord of the Flies, 269
Loren, Sophia, 232
Louis, Joe, 120
Lucas, Frank, 157
Lustic, Victor, 150

MacGyver, 179, 184
MacLaine, Shirley, 252, 253
Magnificent Seven, 25
Magnum P.I., 170
The Maltese Falcon, 20
The Man Show, 170
Manson, Charles, 186
Marathon Man, 29
Marines, 97, 154
Married with Children, 172, 184
Martin, Steve, 34
Mary I, Queen, 246
Mary Tyler Moore Show, 244
*M*A*S*H*, 180
Matrix, 15, 17
McConaughey, Matthew, 18
McDaniel, Hattie, 234
McGraw, Tug, 59
McQueen, Steve, 17, 34, 265
Meadows, Tim, 174
Meredith, Burgess, 182
Miami Vice, 185
Michelangelo, 150
Military ranks, 149
Military salute, 152, 154
Miller, Barney, 170
Miscellany, 261–91
Miscellany Answer Key, 286–91
Mission Impossible, 185
Modine, Matthew, 16
Monday Night Football, 175, 178
The Monkees, 186
Monroe, Marilyn, 44, 115, 234
Moore, Mary Tyler, 244
Moran, Bugs, 143
Motorcycles, 211–12, 215, 217, 272
Movies, 11–40
Movies Answer Key, 36–40

Moving Pictures, 217
MTV, 186
Murphy, Eddie, 21, 34
Murray, Bill, 15, 22, 31
MVP awards, 42–43, 45, 47, 53

NASCAR, 45, 118, 203, 206
Newman, Paul, 23, 24, 27
1984, 269
Nixon, Julie, 281
Nixon, Richard, 281

Ochocinco, Chad, 61
Olivier, Laurence, 29
Olmstead, Kevin, 177
Olympics, 49, 60, 65, 233
Once Upon a Time in the West, 19
O'Neal, Shaquille, 111
O'Neal, Steve, 46
Open Range, 19
Oscars, 20, 31, 234, 252
Othello, 236

Pacino, Al, 13, 15
Page, Jimmy, 270
Palahniuk, Chuck, 187
Parker, Robert B., 284
Parker, Trey, 176
Parton, Dolly, 252
The Partridge Family, 243
Perfect Strangers, 185
Pesci, Joe, 29
The Pink Panther, 30
Pirates, 140, 154
Pistone, Joe, 143
Pizza, 79, 82, 92
Planes, Trains and Automobiles, 220
Planets, 269, 282
Playboy, 264, 265
Predator, 34
Presidents, 138–42, 152–59, 189, 281
Presley, Elvis, 118
The Price Is Right, 177, 186
The Professional, 12
Pulitzer Prize, 150, 238
Pulp Fiction, 17

Quayle, Dan, 244

Racing. *See* Auto racing; Horse racing
Raging Bull, 17
Railroads, 121–22, 201–2, 221
Rambo, 25
Rations, 73–103
Rations Answer Key, 98–103
Reagan, Ronald, 139
Redford, Robert, 27
Reeves, Keanu, 15
Reiner, Rob, 179
Remembrance of Things Past, 124
Reservoir Dogs, 18, 31
Restaurants, 78–82, 85, 89–92, 96
Ripken, Cal, Jr., 51
The Road Warrior, 14, 26, 207, 211
Robinson, Jackie, 115
The Rockford Files, 179, 205
Rocky, 16
Rodriguez, Robert, 44
Roe v. Wade, 235
Rolle, Esther, 243
Rommel, Erwin, 156
Ronin, 26
Roosevelt, Franklin D., 95, 189
"Rough Riders," 142
Ruth, Babe, 44, 64
Ryan, Nolan, 58
Ryan, Wesley, 146

Sabin, Albert, 158
Salinger, J. D., 140
Sandwiches, 79, 80, 82, 84, 86
Sanford and Son, 183
Saturday Night Live, 174, 188, 242
Saving Private Ryan, 12, 146
Scarface, 13, 115
Schwarzenegger, Arnold, 29, 34
Score, calculating, 10, 293–95
Scorsese, Martin, 26
Scott, Ridley, 149
Scott, Willard, 90
Seagal, Steven, 32
Sedaka, Neil, 247
Seinfeld, 171, 177, 178, 181, 190, 191
Selleck, Tom, 170

Semper Fidelis, 154
Seven Wonders, 153, 276
Shaft, 21, 32
Shakespeare, William, 236
Sharks, 106, 119, 283
Shepherd, Cybill, 172
The Shield, 170
Shockley, William, 155
Shue, Elizabeth, 237
Silver Streak, 204
The Simpsons, 177, 181, 186, 192
Sinatra, Frank, 273, 284
Slap Shot, 12
Smokey and the Bandit, 26
Sniper, 12
Sons of Anarchy, 172
The Sopranos, 17, 171, 180
Sorkin, Aaron, 173
Sotomayor, Javier, 50
South Park, 176, 180
Spiderman, 241
Sports, 41–72
Sports Answer Key, 67–72
Sports Center, 171
Sports Illustrated, 62
Springsteen, Bruce, 174
Stallone, Sylvester, 178
Stand By Me, 26
Stanley Cup, 62
Starsky and Hutch, 210
Star Wars, 12
Stats, 105–36
Stats Answer Key, 131–36
Steele, Alison, 240
Stern, Daniel, 24
Stewart, Les, 109
Stills, Stephen, 248
Stone, Matt, 176
Stone, Sharon, 248
Stripes, 22, 31
Sudden Death, 26
Sullenberger, Sully, 207
Sullivan, Roy C., 125
Super Bowl, 45, 48, 54, 58, 65, 107
Superman, 277
Swayze, Patrick, 15, 18

Taylor, Annie Edson, 238
Television, 169–97
Television Answer Key, 193–97
Temperatures, 110, 112–13, 120
Tennis, 50, 237
Terminator, 14
Terms of Endearment, 252
Thatcher, Margaret, 239
Theismann, Joe, 48
Thompson, Bobby, 64
Thorpe, Jim, 65
Three's Company, 177, 184
Thunderdome, 14
Time magazine, 57, 158
Titanic, 218
To Live and Die in LA, 26, 211
Tomb Raider, 233
Tombstone, 146
Tommy Boy, 32, 219
The Tonight Show, 188
Tools, 109, 262, 266–67
Tool Time, 173
Top Gun, 12
Trading Places, 34
Trains, 121–22, 201–2, 212, 215–17, 221
Transportation, 199–227. *See also*
Airplanes; Automobiles; Trains
Transportation Answer Key, 223–27
Triple Crown, 52, 66
The Turning Point, 253
Twain, Mark, 137, 281
Tyler, John, 158

Under Siege, 32
Unforgiven, 20
The Untouchables, 19, 22
The Usual Suspects, 19

Van Damme, Jean-Claude, 26
Video games, 264, 268, 278
Voting rights, 230, 236, 238, 245

Wadlow, Robert Pershing, 121
Wakefield, Ruth, 81
Walken, Christopher, 25
Walker, Antoine, 59
War and Peace, 124

Warburton, Patrick, 178
Wars, 116, 122, 138–45, 149, 151,
156–57, 160
Washington, Denzel, 157
Washington, George, 152
Wayne, John, 179
Wayne's World, 219
Weapons, 107, 143, 145, 157, 160, 283
Weather, 110, 112–13, 120, 129, 283
Weekend at Bernie's, 33
The West Wing, 173
The Wild Bunch, 19
Williams, Ted, 52
Willis, Bruce, 14, 172
Wilson, Bridgette, 249
Winfrey, Oprah, 252
Winger, Deborah, 252
Winkler, Henry, 215
A Winter's Tale, 236
The Wire, 190
Wonder Woman, 241
Woo, John, 16
Woodstock, 239, 282
World Series, 42, 47, 58, 60, 62, 66
Wright, Frank Lloyd, 186
Wright Brothers, 205, 206, 209

The X-Files, 190
X-Men, 242, 276

Yastrzemski, Carl, 52
Yeager, Chuck, 221, 222
Young, Cy, 42
Yun-Fat, Chow, 16

Zaitsev, Vasily, 149
Zellweger, Renée, 250

DAILY BENDER

Want Some More?

Hit up our humor blog, The Daily Bender, to get your fill of all things funny—be it subversive, odd, offbeat, or just plain mean. The Bender editors are there to get you through the day and on your way to happy hour. Whether we're linking to the latest video that made us laugh or calling out (or bullshit on) whatever's happening, we've got what you need for a good laugh.

If you like our book, you'll love our blog. (And if you hated it, "man up" and tell us why.) Visit The Daily Bender for a shot of humor that'll serve you until the bartender can.

Sign up for our newsletter at
www.adamsmedia.com/blog/humor
and download our Top Ten Maxims No Man Should Live Without.